GROWING
A
WISE
FAMILY

100 Devotionals from the Book of Proverbs

With Questions and Answers

Bryan R. Coupland.
Isa. 41:10

Bryan R. Coupland

Spring Glen Publishing • Debary, Florida 32753-0751

GROWING A WISE FAMILY

ISBN – 978-0-9831235-0-7
LCCN – 2010916409

Cover - www.designbystacy.com
Back cover photo – http://dbrendle.smugmug.com

1. Family 2. Raising children 3. Devotionals 4. Wisdom

Printed and bound in the United States of America

DEDICATION

Solomon said that grandchildren are the *crown* (or button-popping pride) of grandparents (Proverbs 17:6). My wife and I constantly thank our heavenly Father for the gracious gift of our children's children. We share so many great memories together: reunions at Lily Lake, Michigan and Wheatley, Ontario; soccer games; birthdays; and of course Christmas.

Our prayer is that all of our grandchildren will: know Jesus as their Savior; have a growing love-relationship with Him; serve Jesus according to His plan for each of them; find loving Christian spouses; and raise their own children in God's Word as they were raised.

This book is dedicated to our dear grandchildren:
Nathan Duston
Andrew Duston
Anna Duston
Noah Duston
David Duston
Daniel Duston
Willow Calderwood
Abbey Calderwood
Quinn Coupland
Raegan Coupland
Riley Coupland

Blessed is the man who trusts in the Lord and whose trust is the Lord. For he will be like a tree planted by the water, that extends its roots by a stream and will not fear when the heat comes; but its leaves will be green, and it will not be anxious in a year of drought nor cease to yield fruit (Jeremiah 17:7, 8).

ACKNOWLEDGEMENTS

Once this book of devotionals was underway, I was curious how it would work in families with children of different ages. I wrote with ten to thirteen-year-olds in mind, realizing that children younger and older would also be listening. I greatly appreciate the following couples who "test drove" these devotionals with their children, and gave me their feedback: Tom and Danielle Brendle, Andy and Kim Daniels, Lynne Curtiss, Bill and Karyn Kurz, Matt and Elisabeth Nixon, John and Paula Oliver, Bill and Lauri Page, John and Carol Pierce, Alton and Cheryl Shady, Jonathan and Jessica Simmonds, and Don and Janice Woody.

Rhoda Johnson did an outstanding job of correcting my grammar, controlling my wordiness, and smoothing out my sentences.

Many thanks to Andy Daniels for his help in formatting the manuscript, and doing the many other computer tasks that were necessary.

I appreciate Jon Frazier's willingness to share from his expertise in the printing world.

Stacy Edwards (www.designbystacy.com) created an excellent cover.
Thanks to Dave Brendle (http://dbrendle.smugmug.com) for the author's photo.

Thanks to Larry Brown, Patrick Brown, Carol Kaptain, and Chet Plimpton for their excellent editing help.

I'm indebted to Jack Eggar, Dr. Gary Gilley, Bill Hurley, and Rick Schatz for their suggestions and encouragement.

Our three children and their spouses—Kelley and Todd Duston, Terry and Paul Calderwood, and Dan and Kari Coupland—made great sounding boards at various stages of the work.

I couldn't spend the time I do on writing without the sacrifice and encouragement of my soul-mate and spouse, Del.

Finally, there would be no book without the "nudgings" of our dear heavenly Father. May this simple commentary on a portion of *His book* abound to His glory!

FOREWORD

Normally, an author will ask a well-known person to write a *foreword* for their book as an endorsement. Instead of doing that, I asked our three children to write a few lines on what a family devotional time meant to them as they grew up, and what it means in their own families now. Here are their thoughts:

Kelley (Coupland) Duston

Early in our marriage, my husband and I desired that God's Word be the foundation upon which our family would be built. Our five boys and one girl have kept life moving at a busy pace throughout the years. When the children were younger, we provided videos, books, and conversation that shone the spotlight on God as their hero. Throughout their teen years, we endeavored to have a family Bible time. In the summertime, we often heard those familiar words, "I'm bored!"

This year my husband suggested that we each read the Bible first in our morning routine. We would generally sit around the living room reading until it was time for everyone to share a theme or lesson learned from that day's reading. We broke it up with a "sword drill" once a week. I could see for the first time that to suggest a routine did not mean it had to be drudgery for them. Some mornings I came downstairs and my twin nine-year-olds were getting a jump on their Bible reading before I had started the day. Now our eldest is at New Tribes Bible Institute, and we know that this time will implant God's Word into his adult worldview.

I'm thankful my dad has been a student of God's Word, and that he faithfully passed it on to my brother, sister, and me. He and my mom have encouraged our families to do the same. We're looking forward to using this resource in our family devotions.

Terry (Coupland) Calderwood

It's wonderful when you can begin to see that your children are understanding important principles from God's Word. As parents we have so many opportunities to correct and guide our children through everyday life. Sometimes it's easy to think that our kids will just somehow pick up what they need to know about God at Sunday school or VBS. I believe that taking time to have meaningful conversations about spiritual matters helps children sort out and put into words exactly what they know about God. Sometimes these conversations are spontaneous and sometimes they are intentional. Both are valuable.

As children, my husband and I were both blessed with mothers and fathers who invested in us spiritually. Their input had enormous impact on our lives. This gave us the desire to have God-centered family times with our daughters. We want them to know where to turn in times of trouble that will certainly come their way. But also, we want them to know that they are God's treasured daughters above all else.

Daniel Coupland

The day has been busy: breakfast, school, homework, chores, dinner, cleaning up, baths, and brushing teeth. The whole family is tired. At this point in the day, my wife and I would like nothing more than to flop on the sofa and close our eyes in an effort to stop the world from spinning. The easy thing to do is to skip family time tonight, put our kids in bed, and justify our decision with a slightly longer than usual prayer at the bedside. But then two things come to mind.

First, I remember my responsibility as a father to bring up my children in the way they should go (Prov. 22:6). When I—the spiritual head of my home—decide that our family will not meet together to read, talk, and pray, I may have robbed my children of the most important part of their day. Most of the benefits that come from family devotions are not seen for decades. Laying a strong biblical foundation in children takes years, a point I will return to below. But sometimes the impact is both immediate and eternal. It was only last year that one of my daughters made the most important decision she will ever make in her life—to accept God's free gift of salvation—after our family had read about Jesus' death and resurrection. It was one of my greatest honors as an earthly father to pray with my daughter in her room. If I would have made the easier choice to skip devotions that night, I might have missed the awesome opportunity to be used by God to reach my own daughter with the gospel.

Second, I think of my parents and the spiritual heritage that they provided for my sisters and me. I think of all of the evenings we met together as a family to read, talk, and pray. My sisters and I did not always make my parents' decision to have family devotions easy; our silent protests—rolled eyes, crossed arms, and shuffled feet—must have been difficult to endure. But I am convinced that this difficult decision made hundreds of times over the course of our childhood and teenage years, has had significant impact on the way that my sisters and I live our lives as adults. Over these formative years, my parents slowly, patiently, and consistently pointed my sisters and me to God. And while the three of us, like all believers, struggle with our sinful nature, we have never lost sight of the way we *should* go. Developing this kind of foundation takes patience, endurance, and prayer. The decision to meet for family devotions is rarely easy, but its impact may be eternal.

A PARENT'S INTRODUCTION TO FAMILY DEVOTIONS
IN THE BOOK OF PROVERBS

Why deal with the topic of "Growing a Wise Family?" Two reasons come to mind:

1. The family is under constant assault from every possible angle: secular humanism; immoral entertainment; "progressive" government; politically-correct educators; anti-God and anti-family media.
2. A solid Christian family committed to God and His will does not happen by accident. It begins as a tender shoot that will either thrive by God's Word and the Holy Spirit's oversight, or it will dry up and become a brittle and self-focused group of individuals.

Did you know that God appears to have written the book of Proverbs mainly with young people in mind? He understands the specific challenges that boys and girls face every day, and lovingly wrote a book with which they can identify.

God used King Solomon of Israel to pen all but the last two chapters of this treasure of common sense. He wrote almost a thousand years before Jesus Christ came to earth. The first seven verses of the first chapter essentially summarize the book. But if you'd like to memorize one key verse that sums up the purpose, I think Proverbs 9:10 comes the closest: "The fear [or reverence, awe, respect] of the Lord is the beginning of wisdom, and the knowledge of the Holy One [God] is understanding." Simply put, if you want God's kind of wisdom and understanding, you will gain it when you desire to know Him and His Son Jesus in deeper and more loving ways.

God's great love and concern for young people is expressed throughout the wide variety of proverbs—He desires boys and girls to make wise choices every day. He knows they will only be successful in living joyful, satisfying lives when they follow His advice. So, think of these proverbs like road signs along a freeway that say: Men Working! Bridge Out! Sharp Curve Ahead!

You'll soon notice three types of people whose choices are clearly described—and we can learn from the decisions they make and the consequences that follow. There is the *wise* person, who constantly asks God for help; the *fool*, or the person who rejects or ignores God; and the *simple* person, who is easily dragged into sinful choices by the wrong kinds of friends.

Here are some suggestions to help dad and mom get the best use of this book in their family devotions:

1. Approach each devotional with great anticipation, desiring to enjoy each other as you discover the practical truths of the Word. If profitable questions or discussions come up as you progress through a devotional, then stop and spend appropriate time there. You can always start at that point the next day.

2. It's probably best for a parent to read the devotionals aloud rather than your children, so that dad or mom can direct the discussion. If possible, prepare by reading each devotional yourself prior to your family time.

3. There are three questions following each devotional that usually increase in difficulty from one through three. The answers provided are only a resource; feel free to answer as you prefer.

4. Several questions ask for your child's personal opinion on a matter. You might want to ask each child the same question. Their answers may surprise and inspire you with ideas for further discussion.

5. The goal is not to have our children become little encyclopedias of facts from Proverbs. Rather, the desire is for them to understand that wisdom can only come from a deep and loving friendship with Jesus Christ—the source of all wisdom.

Have a wonderful time with God's Word and with each other as you work your way through these timeless truths from the book of Proverbs.

TABLE OF CONTENTS

1. Want To Be A Wise Guy Or Gal?
2. Afraid Of God? Really?
3. Know Your Friends!
4. How Good Is The Guarantee?
5. The Dynamic Duo
6. The Other Partner
7. What Are You Leaning On?
8. A Straight Path Is A Good Path
9. Giving Is The Greatest
10. Can Anything Good Come From Discipline?
11. The Universe—God Made It All
12. Praise Instead Of Criticism
13. There Was A Crooked Man
14. How Can You Watch Your Heart?
15. God Is Looking Out For You
16. Green Sails In The Sunset
17. Nobody Likes Pride—In Other People
18. Liar! Liar! Pants On Fire
19. Stirring Up The Pot
20. Swift Feet Are Not Always Great Feet
21. Don't Scold A Scoffer!
22. Soap Doesn't Taste Good
23. What Does It Mean To Walk The Walk?
24. Love is Like A Paintbrush
25. Gossip—Doesn't Everyone Do It?
26. How To Talk To Your Next-Door Neighbor
27. We All Need Counselors
28. A Line Of Gracious Women
29. Gambling With Your Life
30. Making God Laugh
31. How Is Your Family Tree Growing?
32. When Does A Gold Ring Look Ugly?
33. The Amazing Boomerang
34. A Really Smart Idea
35. Mom Gets An A-Plus
36. Animals Are A Gift From God
37. An Unbridled Tongue

38. Lips That Heal
39. My Way—Or His Way
40. Why So Glum, Chum?
41. When Your Heart Feels Sick
42. A Fountain Or A Snare?
43. Wise Or Foolish? Which Will It Be?
44. When To Save And When To Spend
45. What's A Rod Got To Do With Love?
46. When Cool Means Fool
47. I Like My Way—Even If It's Wrong
48. Sliding Backwards Into Unhappiness
49. What's Wrong With Getting Angry?
50. Is America A Christian Country?
51. A Soft Answer—Not A Harsh Reply
52. Is God Really Everywhere?
53. How To Please God In One Easy Step
54. Why Be A Moper When You Can Be A Cheerer-Upper?
55. Proud, Prouder, And Proudest
56. Trusting God When The Heat Is On
57. The Gossip Test
58. Children, Fathers, And Granddads
59. My Brother, My Friend
60. How A "Scrooge" Met His Match
61. Running To My Strong Tower
62. God Delights In The Humble
63. Whatever Happened To Solomon?
64. Our Plans And God's Goals
65. How Good Is Your Word?
66. What Have You Seen Or Heard Lately?
67. Watch Your Language!
68. Don't Believe Your TV!
69. Think Before You Speak!
70. Arguing With God
71. Be Careful Where You Hang Out!
72. More Than A Football
73. What Do You Mean I Can't Eat?
74. Don't Let Money Become Your Boss!
75. Always Choose The Truthful Way!
76. Every Teen Needs A Coach/Cheerleader
77. How To Have A Happy Home

78. Honey, You're So Sweet

79. You're OK, And I'm OK Too

80. Golden Apples In Silver Settings

81. Check Out Your Heroes!

82. Faithful Like A Toothache And A Sprained Ankle

83. Why Be Foolish With A Fool?

84. Don't Be Like The Three-Toed Sloth!

85. How About Tomorrow?

86. Loving Enough To Be Honest

87. The Ten Commandments Of Good Workers

88. To Be Bold As A Lion

89. What You See Is Not Always What You Get

90. When The Prodigal Son Comes Home

91. What Does Anger Look Like?

92. When A Plan Comes Together

93. Two Brave Women Who Saved The Day

94. Written On The Wind

95. The Book That Never Gets Old

96. What Amazes You?

97. Is Your Name In The Book?

98. What Is An Excellent Wife?

99. It's "Mom" Appreciation Time

100. The Fragrance Of Wisdom

1. WANT TO BE A WISE GUY OR GAL?

To give prudence to the naïve, to the youth knowledge and discretion.

Proverbs 1:4

How would you like to be called the wisest person who ever lived? King Solomon was!

Imagine you are watching him, just after he was crowned the new king of Israel. God says to him, "Ask what you wish me to give you" (I Kings 3:5). Guess what Solomon asked for?

Instead of asking for lots of riches, he asks God to give him a wise heart and mind that would help him in ruling God's people Israel. He also wanted to be able to judge accurately between what was right and what was evil.

Then God promised him, "Behold, I have given you a wise and discerning heart, so that there has been no one like you before you, nor shall one like you arise after you" (I Kings 3:12b). God was pleased that Solomon chose to be wise. This young king was smarter even than Albert Einstein would be, because his wisdom was a gift from God.

In this big world of many choices, there are three valuable qualities that every young person can develop—prudence, knowledge, and discretion—and Solomon talks about all three. First is "prudence"—a word we don't use very much today. It means to make sensible, thoughtful choices that will help you, rather than rushed, foolish choices that will harm you.

"Knowledge" is the second quality that Solomon wishes for all young people. This can be gained in a lot of ways—by reading quality books, especially the Bible; by asking questions of and listening carefully to wise and godly people; and most importantly by asking for wisdom from our dear heavenly Father.

"Discretion" is another valuable quality. Have you noticed how some people, adults included, often act foolishly? They even say foolish things that make others around them feel uncomfortable. To have control over our actions and our words is to show "discretion" or to be discreet.

If the wisest man who ever lived, or ever will live, says that these three character qualities—prudence, knowledge, and discretion—are very important, don't you think we really should stop and consider his advice?

WHAT DO YOU THINK?

1. What would you choose if God made you the same offer that He made to Solomon?

2. "Prudence" means carefully thinking through a decision you have to make. Can you think of a decision you had to make sometime in the past, where you carefully thought about it for a long time?

3. To be "discreet" means to have control over your words and actions. Why is that important for a Christian?

ANSWERS TO YOUR QUESTIONS

1. *Personal opinion. You may want to ask each child.*

2. *Personal opinion. You may want to ask each child.*

3. *As Christians, our lives are not our own. We have been bought for a very high price—the shed blood and painful death of Christ on the cross. Therefore, we represent Christ here on earth and are to be a reflection of Him to the unsaved—just as the moon reflects the light of the sun.*

2. AFRAID OF GOD? REALLY?

The fear of the Lord is the beginning of knowledge; fools despise wisdom and instruction.
Proverbs 1:7

When I was in middle school, there was a bully who terrorized our neighborhood. I often took the long way home from school to avoid his street. My friends and I feared him. We called him the "tall and skinny guy."

Today's verse tells us we need to fear God in order to gain knowledge. But God loves us like a gentle shepherd and a caring Father. So why should we fear Him? How do fear and love fit together? In the book of Proverbs, "fear" does not mean to be afraid, as my friends and I were afraid of that bully; "fear" means to treat someone with "reverence or awe"—only God is truly awesome. When you revere someone, you recognize their true worth and value. God wants us to feel close to Him and treat Him with affection. At the same time, He wants us to realize that He is the all-powerful Creator of the entire universe and the only person (along with Jesus and the Holy Spirit) who has never committed a single sin.

In Psalm 29:9 King David wrote, "And in His temple everything says, 'Glory!'" This means that in every corner of heaven there are created beings, including angels, who are constantly praising God for His glorious beauty.

So, why is treating God with *loving awe* the first step in gaining knowledge? When we respect His Name and His Word, we will pay attention to what He says. His Word—the Bible—teaches us how to live and make decisions every day. Our heavenly Father is serious about the things He has written in the Bible. We will bring glory to Him when we obey His Word.

God wants us to keep asking Him for knowledge about what we should do and how we should live (James 1:5). He never gets tired of us asking Him questions.

Awesome, isn't He?

WHAT DO YOU THINK?

1. Have you ever been bothered by a bully? Tell us about it. Did you ask the Lord to help you through that time?

2. Why is treating God with *loving awe* the first step towards gaining knowledge?

3. Is it alright to keep asking God for wisdom in the decisions we make every day? Does He ever get tired of us constantly coming to him with our requests?

ANSWERS TO YOUR QUESTIONS

1. *Personal opinion. You may want to ask each child.*

2. *When we respect Jesus and His Word, we will pay close attention to what He says. We learn how to live and make right decisions from what we learn from the Bible. Our obedience brings glory to God.*

3. *God wants us to keep asking Him for wisdom, even about things we may think of as being small in importance. He promises us in James 1:5 that He will never get mad at us for depending on Him too much. Awesome, isn't He?*

3. KNOW YOUR FRIENDS!

Hear, my son, your father's instruction, and do not forsake your mother's teaching...My son, if sinners entice you, do not consent...My son, do not walk in the way with them. Keep your feet from their path.
Proverbs 1:8, 10, 15

You and I can hear a lot of wrong information. For example, family sit-coms on TV often show children who think their parents know very little, especially anything that's up-to-date. But I frequently meet young people who love and respect their moms and dads, and still ask for their advice, even when they become adults.

Usually parents have gained some of their wisdom by going through hard testings and making mistakes. Bumps and bruises can be a part of receiving knowledge, and your parents would like to help you avoid some of those same hurts. So, be sure to talk with your mom and dad about important matters. You will still have to make the final decisions yourself.

Choosing friends is one of those important decisions. Sometimes children don't understand why. In my growing up years, I had friends at different times who encouraged me to do wrong things—I'm sure I didn't help them either. We made wrong decisions together that could have changed my life for the worse.

At the time, I couldn't see the negative impact these friends had on my life, but my parents did. They took time to show me the importance of friends who could be a positive influence on me, and not ones who could lead to my destruction. King Solomon said, "For the waywardness of the naïve [inexperienced] shall kill them, and the complacency [self-satisfaction] of fools shall destroy them" (Proverbs 1:32).

I'm so thankful that God gave me parents who loved me enough to point me in the right direction concerning friends.

WHAT DO YOU THINK?

1. Why do you think our parents can be a big help to us in choosing our friends?

2. Why does God care what our friends are like?

3. What do you think of this statement: "I'm friends with some kids at school who don't have good reputations so I can be a positive influence on them"?

ANSWERS TO YOUR QUESTIONS

1. *Parents have had a lot of different kinds of friends, both good and bad, and have watched other people's relationships. Your mom and dad have probably experienced hard testings concerning friendships, and they can spare you a lot of pain by giving you wise counsel.*

2. *Because God loves you so much, He is interested in everything that affects you. If He knows a certain kind of friend is going to be harmful to you, He will be faithful to speak to your heart about ending that relationship.*

3. *That may sound good, but it can often be an excuse to do things you know would not please the Lord or your parents. Our heavenly Father tells us in His Word to not make close friendships with people who choose to disobey Him. We can still be kind to them without becoming best buddies.*

4. HOW GOOD IS THE GUARANTEE?

*For the Lord gives wisdom; from His mouth come knowledge and
understanding. He stores up sound wisdom for the upright; He is
a shield to those who walk in integrity...to deliver you from the
way of evil, from the man who speaks perverse things.*
Proverbs 2:6, 7, 12

In today's verses God is giving us a guarantee. Because God
says it, you know it's true. His Word is the best warranty ever.

What does God guarantee? When we prayerfully ask Him for
wisdom in making a decision, He promises to help us and guide
us. He won't force His knowledge on anyone, but when we ask
Him for help, He is right there.

God's guarantee includes four promises:

1. God *stores up* wisdom and discernment for those who love
   Him and ask for His help. Imagine a huge room in heaven
   with lots of shelves—all alphabetical, of course. And there
   under your name and mine is a stack of God's help, ready to
   share with us when we need it. But in actual fact, the Lord
   Himself is our help.

2. God promises to be our "shield"—above, below, in back, and
   in front—even on our sides. When we ask Him to be our
   shield and then wait on Him for the answer, He will protect
   us from danger and help us make wise decisions.

3. God guarantees that He will "deliver you from the way of
   evil." Sometimes without realizing it, we walk into situations
   that are just plain bad and hurtful. Can we avoid these traps?
   Yes! God has promised to rescue us.

4. God has promised to help us when Satan tries to deceive us.
   Some people cleverly disguise wrong things to make them
   look very attractive. Satan is famous for that. But God
   guarantees that when we ask Him to help us, He will expose
   those wrong things and show us the right choice to make.

WHAT DO YOU THINK?

1. What does God mean when He says He will be our "shield"?

2. God also promises to deliver us from the way of evil. Can you think of a time when God clearly kept you from doing something wrong that would have hurt you or others?

3. Let's memorize all four of God's promises to His children. He will,
    - Store up wisdom
    - Be our shield
    - Deliver us from evil
    - Help us recognize Satan's traps

ANSWERS TO YOUR QUESTIONS

1. *God promises to not only shield us at times from dangers that could hurt us, but also promises to shield us from making wrong—even sinful—decisions.*

2. *Personal opinion. You may want to ask each child.*

3. *The best help for memorization is "repetition."*

5. THE DYNAMIC DUO

Do not let kindness and truth leave you; bind them around your neck, write them on the tablet of your heart. So you will find favor and good repute [a good name] in the sight of God and man.

Proverbs 3:3, 4

Do you know someone who is so warm and loving that whenever you meet them you just want to give them a hug? They smile even when things are hard; there's a brightness about them that draws you like a magnet.

That's how I describe kind people. "Kindness" is the first partner mentioned in today's verse. (We'll talk about the other one of the "dynamic duo" in our next devotional.) Lance Latham, the co-founder of the AWANA program, was that type of Christian man. Whenever he talked with you, his face lit up like a warm light and his smile rarely left his face. You just loved being with him.

I think Jesus was like that when He lived on earth, because kindness is one of His qualities. People become genuinely kind when they spend time with our heavenly Father. They reflect the kindness of Jesus just like the moon reflects light from the sun.

Each of us has a different personality, but we can all be kind. We can choose to be kind like Jesus in what we do and what we say; or we can choose to be unkind by saying or doing things that hurt other people. Whichever attitude we choose will likely become a habit.

Do you hear young people and adults making unkind remarks to others? How does it make you feel? If you draw it to their attention, they might say, "I was only kidding" (See Proverbs 26:19). Such unkind talking does not make people bleed on the outside, but it makes their heart ache inside.

Kindness, on the other hand, makes people feel good and positive about themselves and about life in general. Can you imagine a world where everyone is kind and only says positive things to everyone else? That sounds to me like heaven.

Which attitude—kindness or criticism—pleases Jesus? Yes, kindness! Isn't that enough of a reason to speak kindly to other people?

WHAT DO YOU THINK?

1. How do kind people make you feel?

2. What are two ways we can show kindness to other people?

3. Can you think of three different times in the Gospels when Jesus showed kindness to someone?

ANSWERS TO YOUR QUESTIONS

1. *Personal opinion. You may want to ask each child.*

2. *We can say kind but truthful things to other people. We can also serve others by helping them do jobs they might not enjoy doing alone. In other words, kind words and kind actions.*

3. *There are hundreds of kind actions done and words spoken by Jesus that are recorded in the New Testament. He healed so many; He miraculously fed thousands of people; and the kindest act of all, He died on Calvary's cross to pay our debt of sin.*

6. THE OTHER PARTNER

Do not let kindness and truth leave you.
Proverbs 3:3

What's the other partner that Solomon tells us is so valuable? It's "truth," and it's very important because it pleases our heavenly Father. After all, He *is* truth! That means that everything that God says and everything that He does is righteous and true because that is His nature. It's also highly valued because it's hard to find in today's world. Politicians, movie stars, and sports celebrities look straight into the TV camera and make untrue statements that both they and we know are not true. They often say one thing and then do the opposite. It's easy to tell lies.

Commercials often shade the truth also. They picture a make believe world where you are told you can look better, have more energy, feel cool, get rich, or have more fun, just by buying their product. Are we really impressed with words like *stupendous, fantastic, perfect,* and *earth shaking*?

Many people believe that it's okay to lie if it will help them in some way, for example, save them money. Does God turn away and busy Himself with something else when we tell untruths that we think will help us make money? Definitely not!

Like kindness, truth is a part of God's nature and personality. John 1:14 tells us that Jesus Christ is "full of grace and truth." Then in John 14:6, Jesus tells His disciples, "I am the way, and the truth, and the life." And God's Word, the Bible, is called "the word of truth" (2 Timothy 2:15).

If everything related to God is pure, holy, and truthful, does He care whether you and I tell a lie? Some people excuse their untruths by saying, "I made a mistake," or, "I just wanted to make the story more interesting." What do you say?

God feels strongly about what we say—He wants us to tell the truth. Because He *is* truth, He cannot have fellowship or friendship with us when we choose to tell lies. He loves us deeply and longs to enjoy our friendship continually. When we are untruthful, it builds a wall between us and God—and that makes us miserable and hurts God's heart.

Let's choose to tell the truth all the time and enjoy His friendship.

WHAT DO YOU THINK?

1. Have you ever watched a TV commercial and wondered if what they were promising was true? Can you think of an example?

2. If you catch someone telling a lie, and they say, "I was just kidding," what have they just done?

3. Is it correct to say that Jesus not only tells the truth every time He speaks, but that He *is* truth?

ANSWERS TO YOUR QUESTIONS

1. *Personal opinion. You may want to ask each child.*

2. *Most likely they have told another lie to try to cover up the first one.*

3. *Yes, Jesus Himself said that He is the way, the truth, and the life. Because He is perfectly holy, He cannot lie. For God to actually be truth means that He is the source of all honesty and truthfulness. He is 100% holy, pure, and perfect.*

7. WHAT ARE YOU LEANING ON?

Trust in the Lord with all your heart, and do not lean on your own understanding.
Proverbs 3:5

If I had a list of my top ten favorite, encouraging Bible verses, today's verse and the next one would rank very high on that list. During the year after I was diagnosed with colon cancer, I repeated these verses over and over. As I trusted God's promise, His Word comforted me and chased away my fears and negative thoughts.

What does verse 5 say? Simply put, God tells us we can choose not to worry or fret about things. He didn't give us a list of topics that we can trust Him with, and another list of topics that don't qualify. Instead, it's as if He is telling us, "It doesn't matter what the issue is—anything that concerns you concerns Me. Share it with Me. Because I love you so much, I'm here to help you with even the tiniest thing."

Sometimes, God helps us even when we don't ask Him. But it's so much better to rely on Him from the beginning. I believe we glorify Him more when we turn to Him quickly, and glorifying Him is what life is all about.

I have to admit that when I run into a scary situation, my first reaction is, "How am I going to get out of this?" Instead of asking the Lord for help, I try to remember how I handled this kind of problem before. The Bible calls this "leaning on your own understanding." But then I remember today's verse and I quietly pray in my mind something like, "Father God, I'm really worried about this situation. I started to try to figure out what to do on my own, and then You reminded me of this verse. I'm going to turn my problem over to You rather than try to figure it out myself. Thank You for being willing to work this matter out for Your glory and my best."

Aren't we fortunate to have a caring heavenly Father like that?

WHAT DO YOU THINK?

1. What does it mean "to lean on your own understanding"?

2. When you get into a difficult situation, do you first of all think back over your own experience and try to remember how you solved it before? Can you share an example with us?

3. Please read James 1:5 and explain it in your own words.

ANSWERS TO YOUR QUESTIONS

1. *To lean on your own understanding means to depend on your own experience and knowledge, apart from checking with God or even your parents.*

2. *Personal opinion. You may want to ask each child.*

3. *Personal opinion. Make sure the children understand the four main themes of this verse: We lack wisdom; we ought to ask God for His wisdom; He gives it freely and never scolds us for coming; and He promises to give us His wisdom.*

8. A STRAIGHT PATH IS A GOOD PATH

In all your ways acknowledge Him, and He will make your paths straight.

Proverbs 3:6

One of the things I love about God is that He is not afraid to commit Himself. He likes to use the word "all" and when He says it, He means it. Not like TV commercials, for example, that promise to wash *all* of the dirt out of our socks, using adjectives like *amazing* and *unbelievable*. These words sound false and we soon ignore them.

In the previous verse, the Lord encourages us to trust Him "with all your heart." In today's verse, He urges us to acknowledge Him or ask Him about "all your ways." Will He brush us aside if He feels something seems too small? Not according to this verse—we're to turn to Him in all things.

What does our Father promise when we choose to trust and commit everything to Him? He promises to make our paths straight. And what's so great about that?

Think about this. When I was in college, I remember going hunting for mountain sheep and bear on the Alberta-British Columbia border, in Western Canada. A cowboy/classmate friend arranged the whole trip—even a horse for each of the six of us. We camped in the foothills of the Rocky Mountains and spent most of our time on horseback, riding roads up the sides of low mountains. The trails we followed were called *switchbacks* because they zigged and zagged back and forth like a long string of "Z's." We would ride for quite a while, and when we looked back over our shoulders, we discovered that we had made little progress upward. That was because we were not on a straight path.

When we bring all of our needs—gigantic or small—to our dear Father, He promises to show us what is best for us and what will glorify Him. In other words, He will make our paths straight. Another version of the Bible says, "He will direct your paths." (KJV)

So, why go back and forth like we are on a switchback, not making much forward progress? Why not ask our dear Lord Jesus for His help?

WHAT DO YOU THINK?

1. In how many of our ways, decisions, and choices does today's verse say we should ask God for His help?

2. What does God promise us if we will ask Him for guidance?

3. Explain why a "straight" path and a "crooked" path are good examples of "clear direction" and "confusing direction."

ANSWERS TO YOUR QUESTIONS

1. *We should ask God for help in "all" of our ways, decisions, and choices. He never gets weary hearing from us.*

2. *God promises that if we ask Him for His help, He will make our way "straight," or in other words, direct us according to His will.*

3. *A straight path is direct. It doesn't go off in various directions, and take us longer to get to our destination. When we run our own lives, or take a crooked path, we are often not sure what choices to make—we can waste a lot of time getting to our goal. It really can make for a lot of confusion.*

9. GIVING IS THE GREATEST

Honor the Lord from your wealth, and from the first of all your produce.

Proverbs 3:9

Do you ever find it hard to give generously to the Lord and His work? I do. Why? Partly because we do not see an immediate return on our investment—results! If you invest in new shoes, you would have them there on your feet. But we might have to wait until we get to heaven to know how effective our gifts to the Lord's work are—for the donor and the one receiving the gift.

Here are a few things that help me in the area of giving:

1. I keep reminding myself that everything I own, including me, belongs to the Lord. The whole universe is His. Moses said in Exodus 9:29b, "that you may know that the earth is the Lord's." King David also said it well: "The earth is the Lord's, and all it contains, the world, and those who dwell in it" (Psalm 24:1). Pretty clear, isn't it?

2. Because the Lord owns everything, then everything I have— including my own life—is loaned to me by God. I am the steward or keeper of those gifts. We have no right to take total control of everything He gives us. Instead, we need to ask the owner, God, what He would like us to do with His belongings.

3. We give glory and honor to God when we give a portion of our income back to Him for the benefit of His work here on earth. Our gift is also a way to worship God because we are honoring His Word and respecting Him as our heavenly Father. All that we have is from God's kind and generous heart.

God is not having trouble getting by financially; He doesn't need our gifts to survive. But when we give generously, we are showing Him our trust, our love, and our thanks. It's one more way to glorify Him.

WHAT DO YOU THINK?

1. Why should I give part of my money to the Lord, when it belongs to me?

2. Which of the following is true: "Giving some of what I own back to the Lord brings glory to Him" or, "Giving is a way to worship Him"?

3. Read the short account of the widow in Luke 21:1-4. What was Jesus teaching in that passage about giving?

ANSWERS TO YOUR QUESTIONS

1. *Everything I have, including me, actually belongs to God, since He made everything. He is the true owner of all things. He gives us the privilege of giving a portion of it back to Him for His work here on earth.*

2. *Both statements are true. Giving back to God and His work glorifies Him, because He asks us to give generously in His Word. It also is a form of praise and worship, because giving to the Lord shows that He truly is God and He is worthy of our gifts.*

3. *Jesus was teaching that the size of the gift is not what is most important, but rather how much of a personal sacrifice is involved. The poor widow had very little to live on, and yet because of her love for God, she gave generously from what little she had.*

10. CAN ANYTHING GOOD COME FROM DISCIPLINE?

My son, do not reject the discipline of the Lord, or loathe [hate]
His reproof, for whom the Lord loves He reproves, even as a
father, the son in whom he delights.
Proverbs 3:11, 12

"This is going to hurt me more than you," some dads tell their
children just before disciplining them for doing something
wrong. The dad has no joy in inflicting pain on the child he loves.
However, I can imagine some child saying meekly, "I would be
okay with us changing places then."

I received plenty of discipline as a child—all of which I
deserved. When it was over, I was flooded with a mixture of
embarrassment and sadness, because I had disappointed my
parents. Sitting on my bed, I would relive the unfortunate event
and realize I had to make a choice:

1. I could shift the blame for my discipline to my parents and
   find something that had to be their fault rather than mine.
   That would make me the *victim* rather than the guilty one. If I
   did that, however, I would not be restored to fellowship with
   God or my family.
2. I could acknowledge what I knew in my heart, that I was the
   one who had done wrong. Then I could swallow my hurt
   pride, dry my tears, and rejoin my family. Every time I made
   this choice, it felt wonderful to be welcomed back into
   whatever they were doing—almost like nothing had
   happened.

Now as a grandfather, I look back and recall having to
discipline my own children. And I realize what an act of parental
love this "reproof" really is! When God disciplines His own
children, He is showing love.

He is not only training us in His ways, but He is also
declaring to the whole world, "These are My children; they
belong to Me; I love them; and I care about their spiritual growth.
I want them to be like My beloved Son Jesus, so when they
disobey My Word, I will be in charge of their discipline."

Although I don't like the idea of painful discipline, I'm so thankful that God loves me and cares about what kind of a person I become.

WHAT DO YOU THINK?

1. Does God discipline Christians when they are disobedient to Him? How does He do that?

2. If God's discipline shows we belong to Him and He loves us, what does it show about our own parents when they discipline us?

3. What purpose or goal do our parents have in mind when they discipline us for being disobedient to them?

ANSWERS TO YOUR QUESTIONS

1. *Yes, because God loves His children, He does discipline us at times, that is, when we continue to disobey Him. Some of the ways that He disciplines us are by withholding finances, through sickness, or by closing doors to opportunity and success.*

2. *When our parents discipline us, it demonstrates that they, of all people in the world, take responsibility for us and for our training. More importantly, it shows they love us.*

3. *Parental discipline shows that they care what kind of adults we become. They know we will only be happy and a blessing to others if we walk with God. So, their primary goal is to point their children to the Lord, and that very often involves painful discipline when we fail to obey them and our heavenly Father.*

11. THE UNIVERSE—GOD MADE IT ALL

The Lord by wisdom founded the earth; by understanding He established the heavens.
Proverbs 3:19

Why did I choose today's verse? To remind you that *everything* in our entire universe, was created by our loving, all-powerful God.

Throughout your lifetime, some so-called "brilliant minds" will try to convince you that our beautiful world along with the whole universe, started with a huge bang. They say that somehow people like us developed through a series of changes that began with slime, progressed to monkeys, and eventually to human beings.

Recently, I saw a picture of a little bird that catches bees in its beak while the insect is flying and even removes the bee's stinger. It has at least eight different colors of feathers—just beautiful! And that's nothing compared to the bird of paradise or the peacock. Only a loving creator God could blend such vibrant colors and intricate designs.

Do you know that our heavenly Father placed the sun just the right distance from earth to give us the right temperature and light that we need? If the sun's distance altered slightly, we would either freeze or burn up.

People who think that our ancestors were orangutans and gorillas are ignoring one major fact. God put a soul and spirit into every man, woman, and child so they can have a loving relationship with Him. He created all humans with the potential to love God and be loved.

When people lift up animals to the level of humans—or downgrade mankind to the family of animals—they insult our great God. The Bible tells us that the first humans, Adam and Eve, were created "in the image of God." All of their children, right down to us, were too. Animals like dogs, cats, horses, and cows were created by God for our benefit and pleasure—they don't have fellowship with God. King David wrote, "The heavens are telling of the glory of God; and their expanse is declaring the work of His hands" (Psalm 19:1).

WHAT DO YOU THINK?

1. Some scientists teach that the whole universe began with a big bang. How do we know this is not true?

2. What is one of the main differences between animals like chimpanzees and human beings? (It's got nothing to do with monkeys having a tail.)

3. As we look up into the night sky, how does it declare God's glory? How about when we watch a spider weaving a web?

ANSWERS TO YOUR QUESTIONS

1. *The Bible teaches clearly that God created our entire universe in six days. He rested on the seventh day, not because He was tired, but because He finished all that He set out to do.*

2. *God, the Creator, put a soul and spirit in every man, woman, and child, so they would be able to enjoy a loving relationship with Him. Animals were created for man's enjoyment.*

3. *Whether we look at the billions of stars, the vastness of the oceans, or the strength of a mountain range, we catch a hint of God's mighty power. The detailed pattern of a spider's web demonstrates God's great imagination and how orderly He is. In the morning, a web can look like a miniature clothes line pinning up drops of dew.*

12. PRAISE INSTEAD OF CRITICISM

Do not withhold good from those to whom it is due, when it is in your power to do it.

Proverbs 3:27

In today's verse, God is urging us that if we have the means to assist others in need with food, clothing, money, and other "good things," we should help them, and not withhold those necessary items.

You may feel that you don't have anything extra to give away to those who are needy. Some good things that we all have plenty of are "words of encouragement and praise." Rarely do people want to hear comments that are untruthful flattery. But when they do have accomplishments worthy of notice, most like to hear the words of recognition. Ultimately, of course, we give glory to God since we know that, "Every good thing bestowed and every perfect gift is from above, coming down from the Father of lights [God]" (James 1:17).

Do you find it difficult, like I do, to look for ways to praise people? What if your brother scores a winning goal in a soccer game? Would it be a good idea to tell him what a great goal he scored—without a follow-up putdown? If I was in the goal scorer's soccer shoes, I would really like that.

Or what if your sister doesn't win the music competition, but she plays her very best? Wouldn't it be a great idea to praise her effort rather than criticize her performance?

And if you tell your mom after supper that the meal really tastes great and you thank her, will it put a smile on her face? Probably—after she recovers from fainting.

God is telling us to look for opportunities to thank people and give them praise when they deserve it. The devil would tell you it's not cool to give other people encouragement, but then who asked the devil anyway?

WHAT DO YOU THINK?

1. Tell us about a time when someone criticized something you did or said—maybe someone at school.

2. There is an old saying, "If you can't say something nice about a person, then don't say anything." Is that a good idea and if so, why?

3. What does it mean to "encourage other people" with our words?

ANSWERS TO YOUR QUESTIONS

1. *Personal opinion. You may want to ask each child.*

2. *Yes, that is a good saying because it agrees with God's Word: "But now you also, put them all aside: anger, wrath, malice [the desire to hurt others], slander [hurtful gossip] and abusive [critical] speech from your mouth" (Colossians 3:8). One of our goals as Christians is to build each other up into mature believers. Honest and gracious comments help greatly in this.*

3. *When we truthfully focus on a person's positive qualities, we usually encourage them. As Christians, there are so many good things we can say about each other.*

13. THERE WAS A CROOKED MAN

For the crooked man is an abomination to the Lord; but He is intimate with the upright. The curse of the Lord is on the house of the wicked, but He blesses the dwelling of the righteous.
Proverbs 3:32, 33

"Crooked." What picture do you see? Maybe, like me, you see tree branches, roads, and rivers that change direction. Crooked people, which today's verse refers to, usually change direction and act dishonestly, doing anything that helps them reach their selfish goals.

God describes the actions of a crooked or wicked person as an "abomination" to Him, and He will curse their household. How bad is that?

The dictionary defines "abomination" as something deserving great hatred and disgust. Would you want the God and Creator of the universe—with whom you are going to spend all eternity—to feel disgust and hatred toward the way you act? In that Jesus suffered all the pain and agony of dying on the cross *for you and for me*, why would we ever want Him to feel that way about our actions?

What kinds of actions could be described as crooked? Have you ever lied about something to your parents? That's crooked! How about getting angry at your brother or sister because they used something of yours without asking you first? When they brought it back, you chewed them out big time with angry comments. Could that be crooked? Yes, I think so. Jesus grew up in a home with brothers and sisters, but I can't picture Him ever reacting to them that way.

We often ignore our own bad attitudes when we feel that others have wronged us and treated us badly. But then we end up acting just as wrong as the other person—which means that we have both acted *crookedly*.

What's the better way? Today's verse says that God is intimate or very close to us when we are upright or choose to do the right thing. Which do you prefer—to have the Lord be close to you and bless you for choosing to be kind to others, or to have your actions be an abomination to Him?

WHAT DO YOU THINK?

1. What does it mean to be "crooked" and "upright?"

2. Can we be a Christian and still do "crooked" things and have "crooked" attitudes? If so, what can we do about it?

3. To be "upright" means to obey God and seek to please Him. What do you think it means that God is "intimate" with such a person?

ANSWERS TO YOUR QUESTIONS

1. *To be crooked is to act dishonestly; to be constantly changing direction and to selfishly act only for your own benefit. When young people say angry, hurtful words to their brothers and sisters, or lie to their parents, they are also being crooked. To be upright is to follow God's Word in your attitudes and actions.*

2. *Yes, it's possible for Christians to act in crooked ways or have crooked attitudes. At those times, we need to confess our sins to God like 1 John 1:9 teaches, and accept His forgiveness. Then, we need to ask Him for the strength not to do that crooked action again.*

3. *God loves all His children the same amount. However, when we choose to obey Him and follow His Word, it pleases Him, and He will then teach us more about His greatness and beauty. This is what intimacy with God means.*

14. HOW CAN YOU WATCH YOUR HEART?

Watch over your heart with all diligence, for from it flow the springs of life.

Proverbs 4:23

How can anyone even see their heart, let alone keep a diligent watch over it? Well, obviously we can't. Today's verse is not referring to the organ inside you that goes lub-dub all day and night, and pumps blood all through your body.

The Bible often uses the word "heart" to refer to the part of your being that is the real *you*. It's where you think about things, where you feel emotions like sadness and joy, and where you connect with God and grow in your love for Him.

If this spiritual heart can't be seen with an X-ray, and no one—not even a doctor—can tell us exactly where it is in our body, how are we supposed to take such good care of it? I believe the first step is to ask God for His help because we are so easily tricked. Our heavenly Father has perfect wisdom, so we would be foolish not to ask for His assistance. Besides that, He invites us to come to Him at any time. He will never send us away because He is too busy (Proverbs 3:5-6, James 1:5). Also, the Holy Spirit teaches and corrects us according to the Word of God (2 Timothy 3:16).

What's the main reason to keep our heart with all diligence or care? Because that's where we do all of our deciding—either to do what will please our heavenly Father, or to sin and sadden Him. God compares our hearts to a spring that keeps water bubbling up out of the ground. We keep making decisions all day long that are either glorifying to God or very hurtful to Him.

How is your heart doing today? Are you watching over it with all diligence?

WHAT DO YOU THINK?

1. When God talks about your "heart," what part of you is He usually talking about?

2. If God says Christians are supposed to watch over their hearts, how do we know if our heart is in *good* spiritual condition or *bad*?

3. If our heart is in bad condition as a result of sinning against God, what can we do to please Him?

ANSWERS TO YOUR QUESTIONS

1. *When God talks about your heart, He is referring to the real "you". In your heart you think about things and make decisions—you feel emotions like love, joy, and sadness. It's also where you connect with God.*

2. *The best way to know the spiritual condition of our heart is to ask God, since He constantly watches this part of us (Romans 8:27). He is well able to show us clearly how we are doing in our heart, but He will often wait for us to ask Him.*

3. *The Bible teaches that we should confess to God any sin we are aware of, and ask Him to give us the strength to walk in His will. This is different from what some people say, who tell us that if the Lord shows us that our hearts are in bad condition, we need to "try harder" to do what's right.*

15. GOD IS LOOKING OUT FOR YOU

For the ways of a man are before the eyes of the Lord, and He watches all his paths.
Proverbs 5:21

Before I became a missionary, I worked as a staff veterinarian at Michigan State University's College of Veterinary Medicine. I treated lots of small animals like dogs and cats—to prevent them from getting sick, and also to make them better when they were hurt or ill. Occasionally, "leader dogs" would be brought to the clinic, because the headquarters for an organization called "Leader Dogs for the Blind" was in Rochester, Michigan.

While driving through Rochester, we would often see a trainer working with a German shepherd or Labrador retriever on a leash. These wonderful animals learn to watch when the traffic stops and then lead the trainer or their blind master safely across the street. What trust and friendship develop between the disabled owner and their *canine eyes!*

Today's verse gives us wonderful news about God's loving protection over His dear children. When we belong to Him, our Savior says He sees every single step we take. He also sees us when we're standing still or when we're sleeping at night. The Lord watches all our paths. How safe does that make you feel?

Because God knows everything about this very moment as well as every moment in the future, He is able to guide us in ways that will help us. He doesn't want us to mess up our lives.

I don't know about you, but I'm happy to have my heavenly Father watching all the paths that lie before me. Because He loves me, I'm confident that He is not going to lead me into ways that are harmful to me and disappointing to Him. Here is a wonderful promise: "The steps of a man are established [planned] by the Lord; and He [God] delights in his [the Christian's] way. When he falls, he shall not be hurled headlong [or crash, wipe out]; because the Lord is the One who holds his hand" (Psalm 37:23, 24).

The next time you see a blind person walking down the street holding their leader dog with a leash, remember that God sees

45

everything that lies ahead of you and promises to watch all of your paths.

WHAT DO YOU THINK?

1. Have you ever seen a "leader dog" guiding a blind person? Do you remember what thoughts you had about it at the time?

2. As you read over today's verse, how would you say it in your own words?

3. Please read Psalm 23:1-3. How does a leader dog remind us of God, the Good Shepherd?

ANSWERS TO YOUR QUESTIONS

1. *Personal opinion. You may want to ask each child.*

2. *Personal opinion. You may want to ask each child.*

3. *Here are some ways that leader dogs reminds us of God, from Psalm 23:2, 3:*
   - *God leads us beside quiet waters or in other words, to attitudes of peace and rest. Leader dogs lead their owners safely through difficult places.*
   - *Our Good Shepherd guides us in the paths of righteousness or in ways that please Him. The owner of the leader dog puts his trust in his canine guide to be his eyes for him. They become very close friends over time.*

16. GREEN SAILS IN THE SUNSET

Go to the ant, O sluggard [lazy person], observe her ways and be wise, which, having no chief, officer or ruler, prepares her food in the summer, and gathers her provision in the harvest.
Proverbs 6:6-8

The first time I saw them I could hardly believe my eyes. After we had lived in Panama for a few months, we began to see them all over. On an open piece of ground, we would suddenly notice a line of what looked like tiny sail boats with green sails about one centimeter in size. The sails looked like pieces of leaves—because that's exactly what they were. Cutter ants were carrying leaf fragments back to their nests.

You had to look closely to see the ant under its huge load, but sure enough, there it was walking in a line behind its neighbor. How do those ants know how to cut up a leaf that's just the right size to carry? And who tells them to walk in a fairly straight line back to their home? Our loving, all-powerful God created those tiny, hard working, well-organized insects.

Today's verse tells us to learn from the industrious ant. The sluggard—or lazy person—especially has a lot to learn.

Have you ever found ants in your food at a picnic or been stung by a fire ant? Have you seen ants building their home? A simple ant hill is a picture of hard work done by a team who all have the same goal in mind. Sweep the hill away with a broom, and the next day it will be there again.

A person who is willing to work hard will never go hungry. That's how ants are. Those tiny cutter ants can quickly strip a bush or small tree bare, because they stay at the job until it's done, and they work together.

Work is a good thing, and it honors our creator God. He tells us, "The soul of the sluggard [the lazy person] craves and gets nothing, but the soul of the diligent [hard worker] is made fat [or, is fully satisfied]" Proverbs 13:4. Which do you want to be—a hungry sluggard or a satisfied diligent worker?

WHAT DO YOU THINK?

1. What is a sluggard?

2. What good qualities do ants have? In what way are they a good example of teamwork?

3. Why do you think God is in favor of people working hard instead of just relaxing and having fun all the time?

ANSWERS TO YOUR QUESTIONS

1. *A sluggard is an older word that means a lazy person— someone who looks at a job and puts it off until tomorrow. This usually means that the job never gets done, since tomorrow never comes.*

2. *Ants are hard working: they work together as a team; they share with each other; they plan ahead by storing their food for later; and they are persistent (tear their house down and they'll rebuild it quickly.) Teamwork refers to a whole group (or family) working together like one unit to accomplish the same goal. This usually involves helping one another to succeed, and being willing to share the credit for a job well done. Team work emphasizes the whole group and minimizes the hero or the winner.*

3. *Here are some possible reasons why God is in favor of people working hard rather than just always having fun:*
   - *It's good for the positive development of our character to experience hard work.*
   - *In many areas of our lives, we have to work in order to receive the things we need for life. We can't just expect other people who do work, to provide these things for us for free.*
   - *When God made our world, He gave Adam and his descendants dominion or responsibility over the earth to keep it in order. It takes hard work for our world to meet mankind's needs. (See 2 Thessalonians 3:7-13).*

17. NOBODY LIKES PRIDE—IN OTHER PEOPLE

There are six things which the Lord hates, yes, seven which are an abomination to Him: haughty eyes...
Proverbs 6:16, 17a

God is love! Isn't that what we think of most when we picture our dear heavenly Father? He is so kind and gracious that we don't associate Him with the word "hate."

Because He is holy, pure, and free of sin, He cannot have contact with anything that is not holy. That is why all humans who ever lived or will live, need Jesus as their Savior—the only One who can take away their sin when they believe on Him.

Today's verse talks about the first of seven actions of ours that God hates. I believe He feels that way about every sin that was ever committed, but these seven sins are like the foundation blocks on a building—almost all sins done toward someone else start here. Remember, God loves the sinner, but hates *all* sin.

"Haughty" is not a word we use in everyday language, but doesn't the sound of it help you picture such a person? It means to have a prideful, excessively great opinion of yourself so you rate everyone else as very low in value and ability. Why does God emphasize pride as being so awful to Him? Here are a couple of reasons:

1. Satan is proud. We read in the book of Isaiah, "But you [Satan] said in your heart, 'I will ascend to heaven; I will raise my throne above the stars of God ... I will ascend above the heights of the clouds; I will make myself like the Most High [God]'" (Isaiah 14:13, 14). Did you notice how many times Satan said, "I will ..."? God wants us to be holy like Him—not proud and arrogant like Satan.

2. Because God loves people, He wants us to love and care for each other. When we develop "I" trouble like Satan, we begin to hurt each other. It's very difficult for me to love Jesus and do what pleases Him, when I'm only thinking of "me, myself, and I," and how I can look better than everyone else. Do you agree?

WHAT DO YOU THINK?

1. God loves the sinner, but hates all_____ .

2. The phrase "haughty eyes" is not describing the color or shape of eyes. What specific sin does the word "haughty" refer to?

3. A proud person thinks about *himself or herself* all the time. Who was the first proud individual and how did they show it?

ANSWERS TO YOUR QUESTIONS

1. God loves the sinner, but hates all sin.

2. The phrase "haughty eyes" refers to an attitude of pride that often involves a person's words, actions, and even the expression on their face, including their eyes. We read, "For through the grace given to me I [the apostle Paul] say to every man among you not to think more highly of himself than he ought to think" (Romans 12:3a).

3. According to the book of Genesis, Satan was the first created being to demonstrate pride in the form of self-centered ambition and jealousy of God. We find in Isaiah 14:13 and Ezekiel 28:14 that Satan wasn't satisfied with being an important angel in God's presence, but he wanted to be equal or even greater than the One True God.

18. LIAR! LIAR! PANTS ON FIRE

There are six things which the Lord hates...a lying tongue...a false witness who utters lies...
Proverbs 6:16, 17, 19

Today's title is something my friends and I would yell to each other when we heard someone tell a lie. We were little kids then, and none of us wanted our pants to be on fire!

Telling lies hurts the liars and the people to whom they are telling lies. It also hurts God's heart. It is number two on God's list of seven things He hates. So we need to listen carefully.

God is holy; He cannot lie. Numbers 23:19 states: "God is not a man, that He should lie, nor a son of man, that He should repent; has He said, and will He not do it? Or has He spoken, and will He not make it good?" So when He speaks, we can rely on His Word. He's not going to cheat us by telling a lie or changing His mind. Dishonesty has no place in His personality. Otherwise, we would never know which of His promises we could believe.

Because the Lord Jesus is truthful one hundred percent of the time, I can trust His Word. He tells me that I will live in heaven with Him forever, if I believe that He died on the cross to pay for my sins, and rose again to give me eternal life. I know I'm safe and secure in Him. God never exaggerates or says something untrue to purposely hurt me.

But I also know that I sin, and sometimes I tell lies. You probably do too. So what should we do when we realize we told someone a lie? Apologize to them right away and admit the untruth. It might be a little embarrassing, but your heart will feel free as a bird. Best of all, you will experience God's forgiveness and He will be pleased with you. However, if you don't admit the lie, you'll become miserable. Down deep you'll know you wronged someone else, and most of all you hurt God's heart.

Let's ask God to help us develop a habit of telling the truth. And when we sin and tell a lie, let's choose to admit it right away. The Holy Spirit lives in each child of God, and He will give you and me the strength to do this.

WHAT DO YOU THINK?

1. What is the main reason why we should *always* tell the truth?

2. Would we be more careful not to lie if we realized that God *hates* lying? Of all the sins, why do you think "lying" is one that God feels so strongly about?

3. What should we do when we realize we lied to a person?

ANSWERS TO YOUR QUESTIONS

1. *The main reason we shouldn't lie is because God hates dishonesty. He is perfectly holy, and so sin of any kind, including lying, has no place in His presence. All three persons of the triune God are honest 100% of the time.*

2. *Personal opinion. You may want to ask each child. The sin of lying is especially awful because it forms the foundation of so many other sins. There is no way that we can grow to know Jesus better, or expect to be used by Him, if we live in an atmosphere of dishonesty.*

3. *As soon as we realize that we have not told the truth to another person, we should confess our sin to God and receive His forgiveness, in the quietness of our own heart. We should then mention it to the person honestly, and ask for their forgiveness. It might be a little bit embarrassing, but that's nothing compared to offending the Lord Jesus Christ.*

19. STIRRING UP THE POT

There are six things which the Lord hates...hands that shed innocent blood... and one who spreads strife among brothers.
Proverbs 6:17, 19

When we hear of "hands that shed innocent blood," we think of murderers who kill people who did nothing wrong, like in a robbery. It's easy to see why God detests this sin so much. He is the One who gives life and takes it away according to His own will.

There's another meaning that may apply more to us. Do we ever make up untrue stories about people and tell these lies to others? If so, we hurt the one we are talking about deeply. It would be bad enough if our facts were true and we were gossiping about them. But by purposely making up untrue stories in order to hurt the person, we are destroying their good name and reputation. That is almost as bad as shedding their "innocent blood." Jesus would never do something like that.

What does it mean to "spread strife" among brothers? In any group of people—a family, a sports team, or several people working together—some are constantly "stirring up the pot." In a family, for example, where there are parents, brothers, and sisters, it's easy to develop a bad habit of thinking up negative remarks. When others make a comment, we quickly pick through our mind for the nastiest reply we can think of—kind of like someone picking through a bag of garbage—in order to cut them down. Why not say something positive; and if nothing positive comes to mind, say nothing?

Making hurtful remarks can become a very bad habit. In the book of James it says, "If anyone thinks himself to be religious, and yet does not bridle [or control] his tongue [or his words] but deceives his own heart, this man's religion is worthless" (James 1:26).

What we say and how we say it is important, isn't it?

WHAT DO YOU THINK?

1. How would you explain "gossip" to someone who had never heard the word before?

2. When people pass along negative information to another person about a third individual, what do they usually do with the details of the story?

3. Why is gossip so destructive?

ANSWERS TO YOUR QUESTIONS

1. *Gossip is passing on information to another person about a third individual, with the goal of making the object of the discussion look bad. It could be done by just emphasizing negative details about that person, or even worse, by making up stories to hurt them even more.*

2. *They often add colorful but untrue details, either to purposely hurt the one described, or to lift the speaker up as being an interesting story-teller.*

3. *In minutes, a gossiper can ruin another person's good name and reputation that took years to build by passing on untrue or one-sided stories, about them. Nobody wins when people gossip—not the gossiper, not the one hearing the untrue stories, and certainly not the object of the information. Most importantly of all, gossip would be an offense to God's holiness.*

20. SWIFT FEET ARE NOT ALWAYS GREAT FEET

There are six things which the Lord hates... a heart that devises wicked plans, feet that run rapidly to evil...
Proverbs 6:18

Hundreds of cruel dictators and presidents around the world have harmed people, just in my life time. The Bible tells of such leaders all the way back through history to the beginning of the Old Testament. These ungodly men and women did *anything* to increase their own power and wealth. Their subjects' well-being was not important to them—only their desire for more of everything consumed their thoughts.

No wonder God hates these two sins—making up wicked plans and running rapidly to carry them out. In contrast, the Lord Jesus is so kind and caring. He loves all people so deeply that He allowed evil men to kill Him by nailing Him to a wooden cross and piercing His side with a spear. He doesn't hold back His love at all, but openly shows His feelings to men, women, and children.

So how do today's verses apply to us? It's helpful to remember that God is perfect and holy—therefore, *all* sin is horrible to Him. He loves the person but hates the sin.

Let's say your mother tells you not to eat any of those freshly baked cookies with chocolate chips and raisins, because supper will be ready in one hour. But they look scrumptious. So, you look for an opportunity—like when she is on the phone—to take two of those good-looking cookies back to your bedroom and wolf them down. Later, you wander casually back to the kitchen and your mother asks, "Is that chocolate on your face? Did you take some of those cookies I baked for supper?" And soon the whole story comes tumbling out.

Is what you did as bad as what those murderous dictators did? In one sense the "cookie caper" is not as bad because the consequences or results of the sin are not as serious. But from God's point of view, stealing the cookies is sin, and that also hurts His heart deeply.

Let's ask God to help us not do those seven things He hates.

WHAT DO YOU THINK?

1. If your mother tells you not to touch the freshly baked cookies, would taking one cookie without asking only be half as sinful as taking two?

2. When God talks about our "hearts," what part of us is He really talking about? Who do our hearts really belong to?

3. What does "running rapidly to evil" mean?

ANSWERS TO YOUR QUESTIONS

1. *No, disobedience towards your parents is wrong regardless how many cookies are involved.*

2. *Our heart is that part of us that makes us who we really are. It is made up of areas like: our emotions, where we feel things; our brain, where we think things through; our will, where we make decisions; and our spirit, where we enjoy fellowship with God.*

3. *"Running rapidly to evil" means to be eager to commit sin knowing full well that it is wrong and will separate you from fellowship with your Savior. God would much prefer that before we take a questionable action, that we ask Him what He would have us do, and then wait on His answer.*

21. DON'T SCOLD A SCOFFER!

Do not reprove [scold] a scoffer, lest he hate you, reprove a wise man, and he will love you. Give instruction to a wise man, and he will be still wiser, teach a righteous man, and he will increase his learning.

Proverbs 9:8, 9

Have you ever "reproved" someone? What does that word mean? When you reprove people, you are correcting them, or showing that you do not agree with something they've done. It's a positive thing to do, because you want them to recognize that what they did wasn't wise, and it could even hurt them in some way.

But this verse tells us not to scold a scoffer. Do you know someone who is a scoffer? They like to mock and make fun of other people in order to make them feel bad. Wouldn't it be a good idea to tell them that they are hurting other people as well as making themselves look silly? Of course! But there's a problem—a scoffer is a foolish person who is not interested in following God's ways, so they won't learn from being corrected. Instead, they may hate you! Can't you just hear them saying, "Who do you think you are telling me what to do?" See what I mean? They just do not want to learn what is right. They would rather remain a scoffer.

On the other hand, God says that a wise person, who listens carefully to instructions and correction and follows through on what they're told, will grow smarter. Instead of getting angry at the person who gives the advice like the scoffer does, the wise person will be thankful. He understands that this person loves him enough to tell him where they are going wrong.

There is one more important step to really profiting from getting advice and correction. At times, the instructions you receive from others may be hard to understand, and you may not be sure how it applies to you. By taking time to ask God to help you know what that advice means, He will make it clear to you. After all, He loves you so much. On top of that, He has promised in His Word to give you wisdom whenever you ask Him.

WHAT DO YOU THINK?

1. What is a scoffer? Have you ever known anyone like that?

2. Why does God advise us not to correct a scoffer, even though that seems to be exactly what they need?

3. Receiving advice or even correction from others isn't always easy. In what ways will it help us if we encourage our friends to feel free to give us their counsel?

ANSWERS TO YOUR QUESTIONS

1. *A scoffer is someone who mocks and makes fun of other people in order to make them feel bad and make himself look cool.*

2. *The reason why God advises us not to reprove or correct a scoffer is because they are usually a foolish person, and not interested in following God's ways. They will often hate you and become angry toward you—maybe even harmful.*

3. *When we encourage people to honestly share with us, we are being humble –and God says He is close to the humble. When we listen to the advice of friends and even take their comments to the Lord in prayer, our heavenly Father will see that we come to understand. He promises!*

22. SOAP DOESN'T TASTE GOOD

The proverbs of Solomon. A wise son makes a father glad, but a foolish son is a grief to his mother.
Proverbs 10:1

Have you ever gotten soap in your mouth when you were having a shower? It tastes yucky, doesn't it?

When I was about five years old, I got angry with a playmate and called him a bad name at the top of my voice. My mother happened to be in our backyard and heard me clearly. I'm sure all the neighbors did too. Right away she called me home, marched me down to the basement where she did the laundry, and told me to stick out my tongue. She then took a bar of Sunlight soap, which is used for getting the dirt out of socks, and swiped it across my tongue a couple of times. What a miserable experience! I learned a lot that day. I'm sure it hurt my mother to hear me talk like that.

Our parents love us and want to see us grow up to love and serve God, to be kind to other people, and to honor Jesus in how we live. Most parents have learned from making their own mistakes and watching others make theirs, that there is a cost to sinning. When they see us making wrong or sinful choices, it hurts them deeply. It first of all hurts the heart of God, but also causes teachers, relatives, and family friends to turn away from that child rather than be a help to him.

In 2 Samuel 18 there's a sad story about King David and one of his sons, Absalom—a handsome but evil young man. Rather than follow God's ways like his father did, Absalom planned to turn Israel against David so he could be king himself. He almost succeeded except for one thing—it wasn't what God wanted. So the Lord caused this wicked young man to be killed in battle, and David was restored to his throne.

But King David loved his son, and it broke his heart to hear of his death—even though he had become his enemy. David cried as he walked saying, "O my son Absalom, my son, my son Absalom! Would I had died instead of you" (2 Samuel 18:33).

You have a great opportunity to bring joy to God's heart, as well as to your parents, by choosing to be *wise* rather than *foolish.*

WHAT DO YOU THINK?

1. Does soap on your tongue cleanse your heart and your mouth from saying bad things? Why or why not?

2. How have most parents learned that there is a cost to sinning? What does the expression, "There is a cost to sinning" mean?

3. Think about people you have known, both young and old. What are some costly results of sin?

ANSWERS TO YOUR QUESTIONS

1. *No, soap doesn't cleanse your heart and your mouth from saying bad things, because these kinds of hurtful comments come from our heart and mind. Our mouth only speaks from the overflow of our thoughts. Matthew 12:34b says, "For the mouth speaks out of that which fills the heart."*

2. *Most parents have learned from making their own mistakes and also watching others make wrong choices, that sin costs a great deal. Not only does God not bless such actions, but there are often negative consequences you couldn't imagine when you choose wrongly.*

3. *Personal opinion. Some possibilities:*
   - *Loss of friendships*
   - *Family problems*
   - *Financial losses*
   - *Good name and reputation soiled*
   - *People lack confidence in your trustworthiness*
   - *Lack of fellowship with your heavenly Father*

23. WHAT DOES IT MEAN TO WALK THE WALK?

He who walks in integrity walks securely, but he who perverts his ways [or chooses to sin] will be found out.
Proverbs 10:9

How often do you hear the word "integrity"? Maybe not very often, but it shows up in how people live. King David said, "Vindicate [prove] me, O Lord, for I have walked in my integrity; and I have trusted in the Lord without wavering [changing].... For Thy lovingkindness is before my eyes, and I have walked in Thy truth" (Psalm 26:1, 3).

The last few words of those verses explain what integrity means—it's to walk or live in God's truth. That means that all of our actions should be honest and right, in the same way that God is righteous. Some people try to appear on the outside like they are walking with God and doing His will. On the inside, however, they are plotting to do things their own way, even if it means lying and cheating. This shows a lack of integrity.

God understands that humans are not perfect. Both Christians and non-Christians make wrong choices and sin at times. James 3:2 says, "For we all stumble in many ways." But God wants us to choose integrity over evil ways. He even promises that we will walk "securely" when we choose integrity. No, we won't suddenly become perfect; rather we will glorify God by our actions and inspire others to make right choices.

What does integrity look like in real life? One day my wife was shopping in Wal-Mart. She paid the cashier, wheeled her grocery cart to her car, put the packages in the trunk, and promptly headed home. As she unloaded the car she could not find her purse, so headed right back to Wal-Mart. *Someone will notice my purse in the empty cart and steal it,* she thought. But she went directly to Customer Service anyway. Sure enough, someone had seen her purse, realized that the owner had forgotten it, and took it to the store office. Nothing was missing, and the kind person had not even left his or her name. That is integrity in action!

What would you do if a store cashier mistakenly gave you change for $10.00 when you only paid with a five dollar bill? Would you tell the cashier about it? Or would you say to yourself, "Wow! I just made five dollars."

To have integrity you would have to mention it to the cashier. No amount of money can buy a good name. And why not please God while we're at it?

WHAT DO YOU THINK?

1. How would you explain "integrity" in your own words?

2. A simple definition of integrity is, "Doing what is right and truthful when no one else is looking." Can you think of a time when you did that?

3. Mike Huckabee, former governor of Arkansas, wrote a book called, *"Do the Right Thing,"* which is another way of saying, "Have integrity!" Why should we?

ANSWERS TO YOUR QUESTIONS

1. *Personal opinion. The definition of integrity from today's devotional is, "to walk or live in God's truth."*

2. *Personal opinion. You may want to ask each child.*

3. *We should have integrity because it means walking in truth. Jesus said in John 14:6, "I am the way, and the TRUTH, and the life; no one comes to the Father, but through Me." We cannot please God apart from truthfulness.*

24. LOVE IS LIKE A PAINTBRUSH

Hatred stirs up strife, but love covers all transgressions.
Proverbs 10:12

Do you remember the story of Joseph and his coat of many colors? His older brothers were jealous, because they thought their father loved Joseph more than them. Their jealousy turned to hatred, and their hatred made them want to get rid of this favored son. Jealousy causes hatred and strife.

When we read this story in Genesis, we keep coming across the words, "and the Lord was with Joseph" (Genesis 39:2). Even though his brothers hated him, God kept protecting Joseph, because the young man loved and obeyed his heavenly Father.

How does love cover all transgressions or sins? Once again, Joseph and his jealous brothers show us a great example. Even though Joseph spent more than two years in prison, he continued to obey and trust God. In His time, the mighty God of Israel made Joseph the second most powerful ruler in all of Egypt. When a famine or lack of food hit the whole area—just as God had predicted—Joseph's brothers suddenly traveled to Egypt to buy food. From whom? Yes, their younger brother! They did not recognize Joseph when they bowed before him and pleaded to buy food for their families. After all, they probably thought he was already dead.

Joseph, who was in charge of selling all the stored grain, could easily have told his brothers, "Sorry! No deal! Go somewhere else!" Instead, he was honest with them and showed God's love by being patient and forgiving.

After the brothers changed their minds and became humble in their attitudes, the young ruler wept and told them that he was their brother. Did Joseph ignore his brothers' sin? No! He was patient and allowed God to work in their hearts. Did Joseph try to get even with them by putting them in prison or worse? No! Instead he loved them. As today's verse says, he covered their transgressions with God's love.

The apostle Peter, whom Jesus forgave for denying Him three times, later wrote this: "Above all things have intense and

63

unfailing love for one another, for love covers a multitude of sins [forgives and disregards the offenses of others]" [The Amplified Bible] (I Peter 4:8).

What is the greatest example of love covering sin? Yes, it's Jesus dying on the cross to pay for the sins of the whole world.

WHAT DO YOU THINK?

1. How was Joseph able to be kind to his brothers after they had sold him into slavery?

2. When you cover a person's transgressions with love, do you ignore their sin as if it doesn't exist? What would you do?

3. Explain in your own words how Jesus is the supreme example of "covering our transgressions" with His love.

ANSWERS TO YOUR QUESTIONS

1. *Joseph was able to be kind to his evil-acting brothers because God was with him, and he was walking in obedience to God's will and not his own.*

2. *When you allow God's love in you to cover a friend's sin, you are not ignoring that sin as if it doesn't exist. It's just that instead of criticizing them, you show love to the individual by being truthful in a gracious way. You pray for them that they would open their hearts to God, and you don't cancel your friendship.*

3. *Jesus not only "covered" our sins with His precious blood by paying our sin-debt on the cross, but "did away with" those sins and removed them as far as the east is from the west, when we trusted in Him for salvation.*

25. GOSSIP—DOESN'T EVERYONE DO IT?

He who conceals hatred has lying lips, and he who spreads slander is a fool.

Proverbs 10:18

Let's begin with what gossip or slander is; then we can discover how God feels about it.

Scene One: Jeff is talking to Brad, and he mentions something that Mike did. Is that gossip? No! He could be describing how well Mike plays basketball and what a good jump shot he has. He is building Mike up in Brad's mind in a positive way.

Scene Two: Mike shares a secret with Jeff. He's sad about a personal crisis that happened in his own family. He needs Jeff to encourage him, and he expects him to keep it to himself.

Next day after school, Jeff and Brad are riding home on the bus. Instead of keeping Mike's sad story to himself and maybe even praying for Mike's family, Jeff decides to tell Brad—he even adds a few untrue details from his own imagination. The extras are all negative and only make Mike's family look worse. After all, you have to make a story sound as interesting as possible, don't you? No—because that is lying.

Where did Jeff go wrong?

Mike asked Jeff to keep the sad story to himself and Jeff agreed.

Jeff told the story to Brad, and added untrue details; he lied.

Friendships are based on trust and honesty. Jeff broke both of these.

Jeff set a poor example for Brad. He was actually saying, "It's all right to gossip, even if it means hurting your friends."

Jeff is a Christian and Brad isn't, so he is doing a poor job of showing Brad what the Christian life should be like.

What makes the difference between a friendly conversation and gossip? It's your *reason* for sharing the story that makes the difference. If your goal is to make the person you're talking about look bad or make yourself look good and in-the-know, then what you are saying is gossip.

Nobody wants to be a fool, but God says that if we participate in gossip or slander, that's exactly what we are.

WHAT DO YOU THINK?

1. If person 'A' is talking to person 'B' about person 'C', what makes it gossip?

2. Is it OK for person 'A' to add some of his own details about person 'C', as long as they are not negative and make 'C' look bad?

3. If 'C' asks 'A' to keep information "in confidence", what should 'A' do before he shares it with 'B'?

ANSWERS TO YOUR QUESTIONS

1. *You can talk to one person about another person, and it is not necessarily gossip. You could just be talking about some news generally known or even saying something positive about them. What makes it gossip is your motive or reason for talking about them. If you want them to look bad and/or yourself look good at their expense, then it's most likely gossip.*

2. *If what you are saying is not the truth and you know it, then it's wrong.*

3. *'A' should go back to 'C' and ask his permission before 'A' shares the confidential information with a third person.*

26. HOW TO TALK TO YOUR NEXT-DOOR NEIGHBOR

He who despises his neighbor lacks sense, but a man of understanding keeps silent.
Proverbs 11:12

During my growing up years, we had some great next door neighbors. When I was in middle school in Toronto, Canada, the couple in the house next to us had no children of their own. One Saturday, the man asked my dad if he could help me build a kite. Dad agreed. I can remember Bob helping me make a frame out of balsa wood with brown paper stretched over it. I think it was too heavy to get off the ground, but I learned a lot building it. Bob was kind to me.

I've also heard some horror stories about two families living next to each other in constant tension and misunderstanding. It probably starts with something very small. But instead of talking about it in a kindly manner and working out the problem, it becomes like an infected sore. One wrong step piles upon another until a whole stack of hurts and bad attitudes make life unbearable. Soon harsh words are tossed back and forth over the fence until there is nothing but hatred between the two families.

What does God say about that kind of relationship? The person who despises or hates his neighbor lacks sense. We are a dummy or stupid person when we allow bad feelings to build up against another person until we despise them.

This verse doesn't just apply to a next door neighbor, does it? It could apply to any person—in your classroom; on the school bus; or in your youth group.

In Luke 10:29 we read about a lawyer in Jesus' day who tried to trick the Lord by asking Him, "And who is my neighbor?" Instead of giving a direct answer, Jesus told him the story of the Good Samaritan. Jesus' lesson is clear—*everyone* is our neighbor, and therefore we need to always speak to others with kindness and respect.

If we can't think of something kind to say, we should say nothing. We don't want to be dummies now, do we?

WHAT DO YOU THINK?

1. Who does Jesus say is our neighbor? Since Jesus loves the whole world, we should_____ whoever lives near us.

2. We 'are all different, so it is understandable that next door neighbors will have different opinions on things. What should we do when neighbors begin to get angry at each other?

3. As Christians, we have an even greater responsibility for our neighbors. What is that?

ANSWERS TO YOUR QUESTIONS

1. *Jesus said that everyone is our neighbor. That was His objective in telling the story of the Good Samaritan. We should be kind and respectful to anyone we are talking to whenever possible.*

2. *Rather than adding to the tension between two neighbors who can't get along by gossiping about them, we can show kindness and respect to both neighbors.*

3. *We can't force people to get along with each other, but we can show them what a godly neighbor is like. It might even allow us to tell them about Jesus Christ some day.*

27. WE ALL NEED COUNSELORS

Where there is no guidance, the people fall, but in abundance of counselors there is victory.
Proverbs 11:14

I am so thankful for good friends who have kept me from making dumb mistakes by giving me wise advice. One of my best counselors is my wife.

A few years ago, I was determined to buy a truck. I gathered a lot of information about the various models and finally decided on a used diesel truck—about four-years-old—that still looked great. I then drove my wife to the dealership, preparing her along the way to check this beauty out.

On the way home, I finally burst out, "Well, what do you think of the truck?" Her answer was short and simple: "I don't have peace from the Lord that we should buy it."

I was disappointed, but knew we couldn't buy the truck if we weren't in agreement. Within six months, the price of diesel fuel shot up and the U.S. economy took a nose dive. Had we bought this fuel guzzler, we couldn't have afforded to drive it, so it would have sat in our driveway—it was too long for the garage.

Have you read the story in 1 Samuel about the great friendship between David and Jonathan? After David slew Goliath, King Saul became jealous of this young hero of Israel and tried to kill him. David went directly to his friend Jonathan, who happened to be Saul's son, to get counsel on what he should do.

David asked, "What have I done? What is my iniquity? And what is my sin before your father, that he is seeking my life?" (I Samuel 20:1). Even though God had promised David he would be Israel's next king, he was having trouble thinking clearly because of Saul's hateful threats.

Jonathan was able to comfort his friend with these words: "If it please my father to do you harm, may the Lord do so to Jonathan and more also, if I do not make it known to you and send you away, that you may go in safety. And may the Lord be with you as He has been with my father" (I Samuel 20:13).

Jonathan not only gave David wise counsel in the middle of a threatening situation, but also reminded his friend that almighty God was watching over him.

We can't possibly know everything. But we can humbly seek input from others we trust and avoid a lot of expensive mistakes—like buying a truck at the wrong time.

WHAT DO YOU THINK?

1. True or False - It's not good to ask other people for their advice about your life since they can't see inside your brain and therefore can't fully understand your situation.

2. I wanted to buy the truck so much I couldn't think wisely. Have you ever wanted something so much that you couldn't think clearly?

3. Besides Jonathan giving David wise advice, he also reminded his friend of the most important thing of all. What was that?

ANSWERS TO YOUR QUESTIONS

1. *False! Today's verse says that by asking a number of wise people for advice when you have an important decision to make, you stand a better chance of making the best choice.*

2. *Personal opinion. You may want to ask each child.*

3. *Jonathan reminded his friend David that almighty God was watching over him.*

28. A LINE OF GRACIOUS WOMEN

A gracious woman attains honor.
                    Proverbs 11:16

In mapping out our family tree, I've been able to trace some relatives back to before the U.S. Civil War. One thing that stands out clearly is that we have so many *gracious* women among our relatives. I believe that many were Christians who respected God's Word, the Bible.

What does it mean when you say that a woman is gracious? At least three qualities fit this description: wise in her decisions; kind in her relationships with others; and loving toward her family.

At the beginning of the Old Testament book of Ruth, we meet three widows—Naomi, a Jewish woman from Bethlehem, and Orpah and Ruth who married Naomi's sons. How did they meet?

During a time of famine, Naomi and her husband travelled from Israel to Moab—a non-Jewish or Gentile area—and there her sons married Moabite women. Sadly, her husband and sons died. So Naomi decided to return home to Israel, but urged her daughters-in-law to stay in Moab.

Ruth, however, loved her mother-in-law and said, "Do not urge me to leave you or turn back from following you; for where you go, I will go, and where you lodge, I will lodge. Your people shall be my people, and your God, my God" (Ruth 1:16).

So Ruth returns to Bethlehem with Naomi. To provide food for the family, Ruth follows after the harvesters to collect the left-over grain—an accepted Jewish custom. Soon she meets the rich landowner, Boaz, who is a relative of Naomi's husband. He is already aware of Ruth's kindness to Naomi. He said, "All that you have done for your mother-in-law after the death of your husband has been fully reported to me" (Ruth 2:11).

Naomi counsels Ruth in the Jewish custom of how to appeal to the authority of a close relative like Boaz. He already realizes what a gracious woman Ruth is: "...for all my people in the city [Bethlehem] know that you are a woman of excellence" (Ruth 3:11). He decides he wants to marry her, and so fulfills the custom of their day. What a wise woman Ruth was in how she treated everyone she met.

God was pleased with Ruth's ways also. He honored her by making her the great-grandmother of David, King of Israel. See how interesting family trees can be?

WHAT DO YOU THINK?

1. Explain your understanding of what a *gracious woman* means.

2. Even though Ruth was not Jewish, she still followed the Jewish customs when she lived with her mother-in-law in Bethlehem. Was that a good idea? Why or why not?

3. True or False – When Jesus was born, Ruth was actually one of His ancestors.

ANSWERS TO YOUR QUESTIONS

1. *A gracious woman has at least three qualities: wise in her decisions; kind in her relationships with others; and loving toward her family.*

2. *Ruth demonstrated what a wise and gracious woman she was when in Bethlehem with Naomi, by following some of the Jewish customs. If she had insisted on following the customs of her homeland, Moab, it would have been an insult to the Jewish people.*

3. *True! We can read in Matthew 1:5 the list of ancestors of Joseph, Jesus' earthly father, which included Ruth.*

29. GAMBLING WITH YOUR LIFE

The wicked earns deceptive wages, but he who sows righteousness gets a true reward.
Proverbs 11:18

Many dishonest financial advisers were caught and jailed in 2009. One criminal, for example, was caught cheating investors out of fifty billion dollars. He received a 150 year jail sentence for his trouble.

Another adviser, who cheated people out of millions of dollars, tried to pretend he died in order to avoid jail. He flew his own plane south toward the Gulf of Mexico, put it on autopilot, and parachuted safely to the ground, at a spot where he had previously hidden a motorcycle. There was just one problem though. His plane ran out of fuel and crashed in a field in Florida instead of in the Gulf. The police found this crook wet and bruised in a campground, along with his motorcycle. He will also spend many years in prison.

These two men are no different than someone who robs a bank with a gun. Because of greed, they are all taking money or valuables that do not belong to them. They are not content to patiently earn honest wages, but want to get rich quickly by stealing.

What about a young person who sneakily takes money from their brother or sister's drawer, or even from their mother's purse? Would that also be considered "deceptive wages"? Yes, because it's not the *amount* taken that makes stealing sin; it's the *action* of taking something that does not belong to you without the owner's permission.

The other part of today's verse talks about those who "sow to righteousness." Money is not the focus, but rather any activity that pleases God. How do we know what pleases Him? The Bible tells us clearly through stories of men and women who loved God and wanted to do His will—people like Abraham, Joseph, Moses, Ruth, and Daniel in the Old Testament. And in the New Testament, you will meet Christ-followers like Paul, Timothy, Mary of Bethany, and Peter. Their reward or wages will come to them in heaven and will last forever. You and I can also experience that eternal reward. The deceptive money stolen by those wicked men I mentioned earlier has already been taken away from them by the police. All they have left is shame and embarrassment.

I know what kind of wages I want to earn, and what God-pleasing actions I want to make. How about you?

WHAT DO YOU THINK?

1. Which of the following are *deceptive wages*?
   a. A fireman's salary
   b. Cheating on your taxes
   c. Taking some change from your parent's dresser
   d. Earning money raking your neighbor's leaves

2. What does it mean to "sow righteousness"? What exactly is a "true reward"?

3. What kind of temptation do you face when you want to have something right away rather than saving for it over time?

ANSWERS TO YOUR QUESTIONS

1. *Cheating on your taxes and taking money from your parents without their permission would be deceptive wages.*

2. *To "sow righteousness" means to do any activity that pleases God. A "true reward" is one that we receive from God, and it will last forever.*

3. *You could be tempted to steal money or things from someone else, because you weren't willing to patiently save until you had enough to buy that article. There is a great personal satisfaction in knowing that you were able to save sufficient money yourself, and you did it honestly.*

30. MAKING GOD LAUGH

The perverse in heart are an abomination to the Lord, but the blameless in their walk are His delight.
Proverbs 11:20

Have you ever wondered if God actually throws His head back and laughs out loud, like we do when we hear a funny story? Today's verse tells us that God is "delighted" at times and saddened at other times. Maybe He actually laughs when He is delighted.

To understand this verse, we need to know a little about what God's glorious holiness is like. One day Moses made this remarkable request to God—he asked God to show him His glory (Exodus 33:18). Moses loved God so much, but almighty God is so powerful and majestic that no human being could ever stare at Him and live—even though we will be able to once we are in heaven.

So, the Lord placed Moses in a rocky cave and covered him with His hand, so that as He passed by, Moses did not die. Although God is so brilliant in His holiness, today His children who have trusted in Jesus as their savior can approach Him any time they want and talk to Him about whatever is on their minds.

God also loves all mankind, just as John 3:16 says, but He hates sin. It makes sense, doesn't it, that God, who is gloriously and brilliantly perfect, finds sin to be so ugly?

Today's verse makes it very clear that any sin, whether committed by a Christian or an unbeliever, is an abomination (horrible thing) to God. The difference is that a Christian only has to confess her sin to God in order to delight the Lord's loving heart. An unbeliever must first trust in Jesus Christ as her personal savior before she can have that privilege.

When we understand how God looks upon sin, it ought to cause us to think twice before we get angry at someone, or disobey our parents, or tell a lie. I want to delight my dear heavenly Father's heart—and I also would love to hear Him laugh.

WHAT DO YOU THINK?

1. Because God is gloriously holy, all sin—whether by a Christian or non-Christian—is _____ in His sight.

2. Jesus was nailed to a cross and shed His blood to pay for our sin. What does that tell us about the seriousness of disobeying God?

3. What delights God—maybe even makes Him laugh?

ANSWERS TO YOUR QUESTIONS

1. All sin is an abomination [a horrible thing] in God's sight.

2. We can see how serious God the Father sees sin when we realize that because we are all sinners, God Himself, through Jesus, came to earth and allowed Himself to be humiliated, beaten, bruised, spit on, and cursed. Finally he was nailed to a cross where He was pierced by a lance—all of that and more to pay for our sin, not His.

3. Today's verse tells us that when God's people are blameless, or in other words, they walk in obedience to God's Word, it thrills God's heart and He is delighted—maybe He even laughs.

31. HOW IS YOUR FAMILY TREE GROWING?

Assuredly, the evil man will not go unpunished, but the descendants of the righteous will be delivered.
Proverbs 11:21

Someone once studied the family tree of a Christian man who served God faithfully and also that of a criminal. A large number of the Christian's descendants became pastors, missionaries, and full-time workers for God, as well as college presidents, doctors, and other professionals. The criminal's family tree was full of thieves, murderers, and common crooks.

Some people say, "My life is my own, and I intend to live it the way I want. What I do and what I become is my own business and doesn't affect anyone else." Such people fail to realize that the decisions they make and the lifestyles they choose—whether to follow God or a life of sin—will greatly influence how their children and grandchildren also live.

Think of your life as soil in which your family tree of descendants will grow. If you choose to obey God's Word and follow Jesus Christ out of love, your life will be like rich soil that produces a strong healthy tree with lush fruit. On the other hand, if you choose to disregard God and His Word because you want to run things your way, then your life will be like sandy soil with few nutrients. What kind of effect do you want to have on your children and grandchildren?

King David wrote about this same principle in the Psalms. He describes the person who loves God's Word and obeys it like this: "And he will be like a tree firmly planted by streams of water, which yields its fruit in its season, and its leaf does not wither; and in whatever he does, he prospers" (Psalm 1:3).

Jeremiah the prophet observed disobedient people who chose not to trust God. He wrote, "For he will be like a bush in the desert and will not see when prosperity comes, but will live in stony wastes in the wilderness, a land of salt without inhabitant" (Jeremiah 17:6).

How is your family tree growing?

WHAT DO YOU THINK?

1. True or False – The way I choose to live is my own business and does not affect anyone else. Explain your answer, please.

2. Psalm 10:3, 4 says, "For the wicked boasts of his heart's desire, and the greedy man curses and spurns the Lord. The wicked, in the haughtiness of his countenance, does not seek Him. All his thoughts are, 'There is no God.'" How would you explain these verses in your own words, and how would they apply to today's lesson?

3. Why are descendants of a Christian more fortunate than those of an unbeliever?

ANSWERS TO YOUR QUESTIONS

1. *False! The decisions we make and the life styles we choose, whether to follow God or live a life of sin, will have a huge influence on what our children and grandchildren become.*

2. *You could ask each child their own personal interpretation. One application would be the following: The person who ignores God or even says, "There is no God!" may think that their life is private and doesn't affect anyone else. However, if they refuse God's love and live a sinful life, it will definitely affect their spouse and especially their children. Close relatives, business associates, and neighbors are also influenced, both positively and negatively, by how we choose to live.*

3. *The descendants of Christians are born into God-blessed families where love abounds and the joy of the Lord saturates all relationships. It's like a young tree being planted in rich soil full of organic nutrients, as compared to being planted in rocks or beach sand.*

32. WHEN DOES A GOLD RING LOOK UGLY?

As a ring of gold in a swine's snout, so is a beautiful woman who lacks discretion.

Proverbs 11:22

When does a gold ring look ugly? How about when it's attached to a pig's nose? As a veterinarian, I treated pigs at different times, and there is nothing beautiful about their noses. However, God did an amazing job in designing that part of their body.

Pigs love to root around in the ground for food, using their snout or nose. They can actually dig into the soil and turn it over to find some tasty morsel worth eating. The snout is fairly soft, and yet the pig can swivel it around and use it like a shovel. That wet, dirty nose is not the prettiest thing to look at.

Now, what if you attach a gold ring to the side of a pig's nose? (Talk about body piercing!) Would that change your opinion and make you want a pig for a pet? Maybe you could train it to sleep at the foot of your bed. I don't think so! The gold ring would look ridiculous and very out of place.

The real lesson here is not the swine's snout, is it? It's about a beautiful woman (or girl) without discretion. Have you ever been in a public place like a mall, and seen some pretty teenage girls dressed in outrageous clothes, or maybe just not enough clothes?

Or, how about an attractive young mother at Wal-Mart pushing a grocery cart with her small child in it? The child demands that his mother buys him a certain cereal. Rather than deal with the situation calmly and quietly, the mother becomes angry. Her raised voice can be heard three aisles over in both directions. Nobody wants to hear the family's history, but they have no choice.

What do the teen girls in the mall and the young mother in Wal-Mart have in common? They all lack discretion. God created women to be gentle, gracious, and loving. A woman is most beautiful and discreet when she is acting the way God made her to be. What she says and how she dresses and acts, all contribute to her beauty. A gracious and attractive woman will not dress like a clown in public, or be loud and draw attention to herself.

What a comparison! A beautiful girl or woman who lacks discretion and a pig walking around the barnyard with a gold ring in its nose, are both out of place or abnormal.

WHAT DO YOU THINK?

1. What would you think if you visited the county fair and saw one pig with a gold ring in its nose?

2. Today's verse makes it clear that a truly beautiful woman or girl who follows God, has discretion or is able to make wise decisions. What other qualities would a woman have who is truly beautiful in God's eyes?

3. Can you think of women in the Bible who followed God and reflected His beauty in their lives?

ANSWERS TO YOUR QUESTIONS

1. *Personal opinion. You may want to ask each child.*

2. *A girl or woman who follows God's will for her life would demonstrate the fruit of the Spirit: love, joy, peace, patience, gentleness, goodness, faithfulness, meekness, self-control. [NOTE: You may want to discuss what each of these qualities looks like in real life.]*

3. *A few women from the Bible who followed God and reflected His beauty were: Ruth; Naomi; Esther; Mary, the earthly mother of Jesus; Elizabeth; Mary, sister of Lazarus; Priscilla.*

33. THE AMAZING BOOMERANG

There is one who scatters, yet increases all the more, and there is one who withholds what is justly due, but it results only in want. The generous man will be prosperous, and he who waters will himself be watered.

Proverbs 11:24, 25

Have you ever tried to throw a boomerang? It's called the gift you can't throw away. I had always read (especially in comic books) that this curved piece of wood is supposed to return right to you when you throw it.

I first tried it on a trip to Australia, and I noticed that the harder I threw it, the more of an arc it made, and definitely started to reverse its direction. If I threw it with very little force, it would just fall to the ground like any stick.

So, what's so amazing about the boomerang? Well, the harder you throw it away, the more it comes back to you. There are at least three things in life similar to that—the more you give them away, the more you are blessed yourself. I don't recommend you practice them just to get more for yourself, but they are worth thinking about:

1. *Time with God* – According to the Bible, the greatest treasure in the world is to know Jesus Christ. The more you read His precious Word and spend time talking with Him as a friend, the more you will learn about Him and the great things He has graciously given you.

2. *Kindness to Others* – I have noticed that the more people choose to be kind to others, the more they are rewarded with friendship—and we all like having friends. The opposite is also true. The more we talk harshly to people and treat them roughly, the more alone we become. They think, "Who needs friends like that?" As we show kindness to the people around us, they will often want to treat us the same way.

3. *Giving to the Lord's Work* – What does the Bible teach about being generous to people in need? When we choose to give some of what we have to those who have very little, God is pleased and blesses us in a whole variety of ways. That

doesn't mean that we should give generously just so we will get more back. We should always give to please God. However, the Lord promises to bless generous givers in more ways than we can even imagine.

WHAT DO YOU THINK?

1. Please explain in your own words the first part of today's verse, "There is one who scatters, yet increases all the more."

2. In today's lesson, we mentioned that those who are _____ to everyone, tend to be rewarded with friendships. What quality were we discussing? Tell us how you have found that principle to work.

3. What did we say was the result of spending time with Jesus Christ—both talking to Him and serving Him?

ANSWERS TO YOUR QUESTIONS

1. *There is an interesting situation that happens when we give generously—God blesses us greatly in return. Our reason for giving should not be just so we can receive more for ourselves. This doesn't just apply to our money, but also to our time, our love, and our spiritual gifts.*

2. *Those who are "kind" to everyone, tend to be rewarded with friendships. We were discussing the principle of life where the more we give away to others in need, the more we are blessed ourselves. NOTE: There is a place here for the children to share their personal experience in this area.*

3. *The more we read God's precious Word and spend time talking with Him as a friend, the more we will learn about Him and His gracious gift of love to us.*

34. A REALLY SMART IDEA

The fruit of the righteous is a tree of life, and he who is wise wins souls.

Proverbs 11:30

What is it about fishing that attracts people so much? Every day when I drive to work, I see dozens of people sitting along the banks of Lake Monroe. It might be 95 degrees F or it could be drizzling rain, but some folks will be clutching their rods, staring straight ahead, and hoping for that big strike.

I have also seen fishermen standing shoulder to shoulder in a river in Washington State, and I wondered how they kept their fishing lines from getting tangled. When the salmon are spawning—or swimming upstream to lay their eggs—the rows of fishermen are like Wal-Mart on the day after Thanksgiving.

Is it that people like to *eat* fish? Properly cooked fish can be delicious, but I believe it's more than that. There is a thrill that comes when a fish hits your lure and the battle begins. When you finally bring that "big one" up close to the boat and slip the net under him, the joy of victory is hard to put into words.

If you think that is thrilling, you ought to experience leading someone to Christ. Jesus challenged a group of fishermen: "Follow Me, and I will make you fishers of men" (Matthew 4:19). I think the Master was saying, "You may think that fishing for fish is profitable, but just wait until you start sharing the gospel with people and watching their lives change. There's no thrill quite like it."

There are two things we can learn about winning souls in this verse in Matthew:

1. First of all, Jesus wants us to *follow Him*. He wants to be able to guide us like a shepherd leads his sheep, and He desires us to lovingly follow and obey Him.

2. Next, Jesus didn't tell His disciples to go off on their own and start sharing the gospel with people. What He did say was that once His children began to follow Him, He would make them into fishers of men. It's not our words or cleverness that saves people; it's the good news of Christ's payment for our

sin, under the guiding hand of the Holy Spirit, that saves people.

WHAT DO YOU THINK?

1. What does it mean to be a "fisher of men (also women and children)"?

2. What did Jesus ask the disciples to do before they started fishing for *people* rather than *fish?*

3. One of the thrills of leading someone to Christ, is that a person who was going to spend eternity in hell, is now going to be forever with Jesus in heaven. What is another blessing that could come from this?

ANSWERS TO YOUR QUESTIONS

1. *When Jesus invited some of His disciples to follow Him, He promised to make them fishers of men. By this He meant that He would teach them to go out and share the gospel of Christ with unbelievers. When anyone hears the gospel and believes, it's like drawing them into the net of the body of Christ.*

2. *Jesus first asked the disciples to "follow Him", or in other words, to be sure they were believers themselves and walking with the Lord. Then, Jesus would be able to teach them how to lead the unsaved to Him.*

3. *Besides knowing that a newly saved individual now has eternal life and will live forever with the Lord in heaven, it also means that Jesus Christ is glorified and receives praise for saving that individual.*

4. *NOTE: Since today's verse is in the Old Testament and the way of salvation as it appears in the Gospels has not yet been introduced, the reference to "winning souls" may refer to pointing people towards God's wisdom.*

35. MOM GETS AN A-PLUS

An excellent wife is the crown of her husband.
Proverbs 12:4

Do you ever stop to think about what a wonderful mom you have? Because you see her every day, it's easy to forget what a blessing she is to the family. So much of what she does in the home is in the background, and you only realize it when she is sick or away on a trip.

How do clean clothes keep appearing in our dresser drawers? Moms do hours of laundry every week, carefully fold the clean clothes, and put them away. And then there are those tasty meals with our favorite oatmeal cookies—where do they come from? Mom goes to the grocery store and tries to buy delicious food with high nutritional value at sale prices—with coupons no less. All this happens before the cooking and baking even begin.

Did you count the number of times your mom heard you crying at night when you were sick? She frequently got out of bed to take your temperature, give you medicine for your fever, and rock you back to sleep.

There isn't enough space here to describe all the different jobs that moms do to make their children's lives easier. She is the friendly taxi service to soccer games, gymnastics class, or to a friend's house.

And then when Christmas time comes and she opens that card you made at school, along with a 50 cent potholder, you would think you gave her a gold watch. The look on her face tells you that your little gifts are payment enough for all her giving, sacrificing, and loving.

As a boy, I used to grumble about having to make my bed every day. Now when I look back, I realize who kept the whole house clean and tidy, so that I always felt good about bringing my friends home. My mom seemed to have an eye like an eagle to spot any curl of dust or "shoes that don't belong there."

Yes, an excellent wife and a loving mom is not only a crown to her husband, but also adds to the honor and respect others pay to him. Why don't you shock her today and tell her that she is the best mom in the world!

WHAT DO YOU THINK?

1. Can you think of two special things that your mom does just for you?

2. What is it that *motivates* an "excellent wife" to care for her family and serve them so faithfully?

3. What does it mean that an excellent or godly wife is a "crown" to her husband?

ANSWERS TO YOUR QUESTIONS

1. *Personal opinion. You may want to ask each child.*

2. *Moms are motivated by love for their families, but that love, if it's real, comes from God the Father who is love.*

3. *When we read that an excellent wife is a crown to her husband, it means she enhances or adds to the appearance and success of her husband. An ungodly wife can drag a husband down, but a godly, gracious wife can be like a jewel in his crown—or, the crown itself.*

36. ANIMALS ARE A GIFT FROM GOD

A righteous man has regard for the life of his beast, but the compassion of the wicked is cruel.
Proverbs 12:10

Can you imagine how boring our world would be without animals? How sad for us if God had not created dogs and cats for house pets—or sleek horses with their foals at their side. Somehow fields in the countryside would look bare without a cluster of cattle or sheep burying their heads in the grass. I love to watch the woodpecker hammering away on a tree and a hummingbird, like a tiny helicopter, flying in one spot while it draws nectar from a flower.

How do animals fit into the whole order of our world, and what is our responsibility toward them? In the story of creation in the book of Genesis, God says twice that man should "rule over the fish of the sea and over the birds of the sky, and over every living thing that moves on the earth" (Genesis 1:28).

One big difference between humans and animals is that people were created by God *in His image* (Genesis 1:26). That doesn't mean that we are gods, but rather that God made us with a soul and spirit so we can communicate with Him and learn to love Him.

Another major difference between animals and humans is that people are "eternal." That means that even when we die, our souls and our new bodies will live on forever—either with God in heaven or separated from God in hell. Animals, on the other hand, do not live for all eternity after they die—at least the Bible doesn't mention it.

Because our loving God created animals, we should treat them with respect. Some religions in Asia actually worship their animals, but this is not God's plan. In fact, when the nation of Israel did that, God was angry with them.

God designed certain animals to be food for us, like cattle, sheep, pigs, fish, and chickens. Others are strong and can be trained to help us with our work. In all cases, we need to remember that they are a gift from God to make our lives more enjoyable. Today's verse even tells us that people who purposely treat animals in a cruel way do not please God. Being kind to animals is one more way to show Him our thankfulness.

WHAT DO YOU THINK?

1. What is one way that God designed humans differently than animals?

2. Romans 1:25 says that unbelievers have a tendency to worship and serve "the creature" [animals] rather than "the Creator" [God]. What does that mean?

3. Name two ways that animals serve humans.

ANSWERS TO YOUR QUESTIONS

1. *God created humans in His image, or in other words, with a spirit so that we can enjoy Him in sweet fellowship. He breathed into Adam's nostrils the breath of life, but He spoke and animals were created. God created man to be eternal [last forever], while animals are not.*

2. *Many people don't believe in God because they can't see Him. They can see the beauty of animals and nature, and so they begin to worship them instead of God. If you asked such people if they worshipped nature, they would say, "No!", but they devote their time, their money, and their energy to the glorification and praise of nature—something we should only do for God.*

3. *Some animals like chickens, fish, sheep, cows, and pigs provide mankind with food. Other animals like horses and oxen are used for their strength. Camels provide transportation.*

37. AN UNBRIDLED TONGUE

An evil man is ensnared by the transgression of his lips, but the righteous will escape from trouble.
Proverbs 12:13

I wonder why the Lord put so many verses in the book of Proverbs about the things we say—both good and bad. Could it be because our words can either strengthen other people and help them to be successful, or they can hurt them deeply and push them into defeat? God uses terms like "the tongue" and "lips," but they both refer to the words that come from our thoughts. So, if we are saying hurtful, critical things, then the problem is with our *heart*, isn't it, and not with our tongue or lips?

Today's verse says that an evil man, which could also refer to a Christian who is not obeying God and His Word, is "ensnared" by his evil words. This is a picture of an animal that is caught in a hunter's trap, and is no longer free.

A person who constantly says mean and hurtful things to other people can cause deep hurts. Friendships are broken, close family relationships are ruined, and a trail of unhappiness follows them everywhere they go. One day they may stop and realize how many people they have hurt with their unkind words. But because of their harsh and unfriendly reputation, people won't want to come near them.

Governor Mike Huckabee, in his book *"A Simple Christmas,"* tells about his dad choosing not to go to church during Mike's growing up years. He went once, but someone made fun of him for not wearing proper church clothes. He was so hurt, he never went back. How sad that such unkind words could result in a person not coming to Christ. Fortunately, Mike's dad did trust in the Lord in his later years.

In the book of James, God compares controlling what you say to putting a bit and bridle in a horse's mouth: "If anyone thinks himself to be religious [a follower of Jesus], and yet does not bridle his tongue but deceives his own heart, this man's religion [Christian testimony] is worthless" (James 1:26). For a horse to be under its master's control, it must wear a bit and bridle.

In the same way, a Christian must be under God's control in order to draw unsaved people to Jesus Christ. I find that when I am about to say something unkind to another person, the Holy Spirit instantly cautions me not to say it. I can still choose to hurt both my friend and the Lord Jesus—or I can swallow the words and choose to be kind.

God's bit and bridle can be such a help to us!

WHAT DO YOU THINK?

1. Although the Bible says that our tongue and lips can get us into trouble, what part of us is the real problem?

2. What can happen to us if we constantly say unkind and hurtful things to other people?

3. What does a bit and bridle in a horse's mouth have to do with the way we talk to each other?

ANSWERS TO YOUR QUESTIONS

1. *When the Bible talks about a person sinning with their tongue and lips, the real problem is their mind where we make all our decisions. The Bible often refers to the mind as a person's heart.*

2. *If we constantly say unkind things to other people, we can produce deep hurts, break friendships, ruin close family relationships, leave a trail of unhappiness behind us, and develop a reputation as a mean-spirited person.*

3. *A person who rides horseback usually puts a bit and bridle in their horse's mouth to guide and control it. God's bit and bridle in our mouths—actually in our minds—is the Holy Spirit who wants to control what we say.*

38. LIPS THAT HEAL

There is one who speaks rashly like the thrusts of a sword, but the tongue of the wise brings healing.
Proverbs 12:18

While I was attending college, I knew a person who spoke "rashly" sometimes to other people. [*Rashly* means hasty or without careful thought.] At times he would make too quick a reply to people in an attempt to be funny, and his words would often hurt rather than heal. This person I'm talking about here is *me*.

How could that happen? Although I had been a Christian since I was seven years old, in college I became a disobedient child of God and went my own way. I wanted to be liked by the unbelievers around me. So, I chose that path rather than the path of obedience to my Savior who died on the cross for me. I'm so thankful to God that He brought me to my senses after college; from then on I decided to love and obey Jesus.

Today's verse says that our words can be "like the thrusts of a sword." What we say to others cannot actually cut them and draw blood. But we can certainly cut people down with criticism and mean comments so that we embarrass them in front of others and make them feel very small.

How did Jesus speak to people when He lived on earth? When I think how our words can actually heal others, I'm reminded how kind Jesus was to people who came to Him. His loving words always gave people comfort and hope.

Take, for example, the time our Savior was visiting His friends at the house of Lazarus in Bethany. Martha got very upset because her sister Mary was listening to Jesus talk rather than helping her prepare the meal (Luke 10:40-42). She even *commanded* the Lord, "Tell her [Mary] to help me." Rather than rebuking Martha for giving orders to Him, the Creator of the universe, He kindly explained that Mary was doing what was most important—listening to His life-giving words.

The next time you pray and talk with Jesus, why don't you ask Him if your words to other people are often "like the thrusts of a sword" or like a healing ointment.

WHAT DO YOU THINK?

1. How can our words be "like the thrusts of a sword"?

2. How can our choice of words actually *heal* other people?

3. Please explain in your own words how Jesus, by His own example, taught Mary and Martha about using healing words.

ANSWERS TO YOUR QUESTIONS

1. *If we speak critically to people, our words don't actually cut them physically and draw blood, but they can certainly hurt their feelings, embarrass them in front of their friends, and make them sad.*

2. *Jesus didn't use hurtful and critical words with people, even when they were doing wrong. When He corrected others for their sin, He did it in a kind way. He showed them love and gave them hope.*

3. *Personal opinion. You may want to ask each child.*

39. MY WAY—OR HIS WAY

The way of a fool is right in his own eyes, but a wise man is he who listens to counsel.
                                                                    Proverbs 12:15

In 1968, a singer named Frank Sinatra recorded a song that seemed to define his life's theme—he lived it exactly the way he wanted to without anyone else's help, not even God's. The song was called, *My Way.* In the first verse, he declares that his life is nearing the end—the "final curtain." He even congratulates himself that he has lived a full life and done everything he wanted to do. The punch line is that he did it (his life) his own way.[1]

What do you think about living life that way? That would also mean that when such people stand before God one day, they would have to take sole responsibility for their sin and failure to trust Him. Their own confession would be that they chose to rely only on themselves. How sad!

Today's verse tells us that a person who listens to the advice and counsel of godly and experienced people is *wise.* The opposite is also true—those who refuse to seek out and listen to wise counsel are *foolish!*

King Saul of Israel is a perfect example of such a foolish man. God told Saul, through the prophet Samuel, to destroy Israel's enemy King Amalek, his army, and everything associated with him (I Samuel 15:3). Instead of listening to Samuel's wise counsel—really it was God's command—Saul decided to do things "his way." He chose to let the enemy king live along with the best of his animals. Apparently, he felt he was wiser than the Creator of the universe.

The God of Israel was quick to deal with this disobedient ruler. Once again, He spoke through the prophet Samuel, who said to Saul, "Has the Lord as much delight in burnt offerings and sacrifices as in obeying the voice of the Lord?...Because you have rejected the word of the Lord, He has also rejected you from being king" (1 Samuel 15:22, 23). Later, we read that God replaced King Saul with David, who was a man after God's own heart.

Well, are we wise to listen to godly counsel based on God's Word—or would we still like to do things "our way"?

WHAT DO YOU THINK?

1. What is the main problem with always doing things "my way" throughout your life?

2. When we need to make an important decision, what does today's verse tell us to do?

3. King Saul kept alive the healthiest and fattest animals of the enemy, rather than killing them. What's wrong with that?

ANSWERS TO YOUR QUESTIONS

1. *If people choose to do things "my way" throughout their entire life, they will not be able to blame their sin on anyone else when they stand before God. Even their words would condemn them.*

2. *Today's verse says that when young people have an important decision to make, they should discuss it with their parents and friends who have experience and wisdom. In the long run, they will be glad they got some extra brain power involved.*

3. *King Saul insisted on doing things "my way." When God told him to kill all of the enemy's animals, he decided on his own to keep the fattest ones alive. Saul disobeyed God and did not follow His will, which makes his actions sin, and God cannot bless sin.*

40. WHY SO GLUM, CHUM?

Anxiety in the heart of a man weighs it down, but a good word makes it glad.

Proverbs 12:25

Have you ever had something happen in your life that caused you to be very sad for a while? I think everybody experiences that at one time or another. Today's verse describes this feeling as though a ten pound weight is hooked onto the bottom of a person's heart, and it takes extra effort to even beat. It's called an *anxious heart.*

When I was in high school, both my mother and father worked during the day. I had jobs to do at home before I left for school. I was usually the last one to leave in the morning and the first one to arrive home in the evening.

One of my jobs was to put fresh seed and water in the bird cage for our two budgies—a blue male and a green female—and then make sure the cage door was closed. One day, instead of doing my job in the morning like my mother said, I decided on my own to do it after school. To make matters worse, I failed to close the cage door before I left.

Instead of obeying what my parents said, I made my own decision—I put off feeding our birds until after school and so forgot to close their cage door. I would be home first and for sure the birds wouldn't tell my parents. Not only did I disobey my parents, but I put our pet budgies in danger.

When I got home after school, I went directly to feed our birds and noticed right away that the cage door was open. I could only see the green female we called "Mrs. Billy." Where was Mr. Billy, the blue male? I looked all around the living room and finally found his lifeless body in the kitchen. He had obviously flown into the blinds over the window and hurt himself enough that he died during the day.

I was so sad to realize that my disobedience had caused his death. With tears flowing freely, I put him in a little box and buried him in the garden. I don't remember now what my parents said when they arrived home. I think they realized that I had learned a very important lesson the hard way.

There are very good reasons why our parents ask us to do the things they do. They have learned by experience what is helpful and hurtful, and they want to keep us from making the same mistakes they did.

WHAT DO YOU THINK?

1. What does an "anxious" heart feel like? Can you remember having such a feeling? What caused it?

2. In the example of our pet birds, I planned to feed them *after* school rather than *before* I left. Wasn't I still obeying my parents even though I did it later?

3. The second part of today's verse says, "But a good word makes it [your anxious heart] glad." Can you remember a time when you were sad and discouraged, and someone made you feel much better with some kind words?

ANSWERS TO YOUR QUESTIONS

1. *When a person's heart is anxious, it feels like there is a ten pound weight hooked on the bottom of it. It takes extra effort even for her heart to beat. NOTE: You may want to ask each child for their opinion for the rest of the question.*

2. *So-called partial obedience is not obedience at all. My parents told me to feed the birds "before" school and make sure their cage door was closed for a very good reason. I was disobedient, not partly obedient.*

3. *Personal opinion. You may want to ask each child.*

96

41. WHEN YOUR HEART FEELS SICK

Hope deferred makes the heart sick, but desire fulfilled is a tree of life.

Proverbs 13:12

What does it mean for your heart to be sick? Does it mean that it has a fever and has to take two aspirins and go to bed? Of course not! But a *sick heart* does happen to all of us sooner or later.

Let's pretend that you are ten years old, and decide that you love horses so much that you want one of your own. The more you read books about horses and see horsey-type movies like *Black Velvet*, the more you long to ride one any time you want. But your parents know that horses take much care; just feeding them requires a lot of strength. So your dad and mom wisely decide that if you save your money, they will help you buy your own horse when you are fifteen years old.

The good news is that one day you will have a horse that you can ride and care for. The bad news is that you have to wait five whole years for it to happen. That's what "hope deferred" is— you are hopeful that you will eventually own a horse. Your hope is "deferred" or put off until later—five years to be exact.

The second part of today's verse says that your "desire fulfilled is a tree of life," or in other words a great joy. Once the thing you really looked forward to arrives, your heart is no longer "sick," but excited and thankful.

There is a great story in Genesis 29 that describes "hope deferred" and "desire fulfilled." Jacob, one of Isaac's sons, falls in love with Laban's beautiful daughter, Rachel. In order to marry her, he first has to work for her father for seven years. But when the time arrives, Laban tricks him and presents her older sister Leah to be his wife. Jacob still loves Rachel and wants to marry her, even though her sneaky father says he must work another seven years to gain his bride. [Note: In Old Testament days, God permitted Jewish men to have more than one wife.]

I'm sure Jacob's heart was "sick" many times while he waited to marry Rachel. But finally, when he completed the years of work and took her as his wife, his joy and hope were fulfilled and he was a very happy man.

How can you wait patiently for something you really want? The best way I know is to share your thoughts with God in prayer and wait for His answer. He knows the best time to give it to you.

WHAT DO YOU THINK?

1. Have you ever had to wait for what seemed like a long time, for something you really wanted? How would you describe your feelings?

2. What can we learn about "hope deferred" from the farmer who waits patiently until harvest time? Please read and explain James 5:7.

3. Before Jesus' birth in Bethlehem, many righteous Jews like Simeon had waited their whole lifetime for God to fulfill His promise to send His Son to earth. Please read Luke 2:25-30 and explain in your own words what was happening.

ANSWERS TO YOUR QUESTIONS

1. *Personal opinion. You may want to ask each child.*

2. *Farmers know they can't plant their grain seeds one day and expect to see it ready for harvest the next day. They have to wait for the soil, the sun, the fertilizer, and the rain to do their work in maturing the grain.*

3. *NOTE: You may want to have someone read Luke 2:25-30 and someone else explain what was happening.*

42. A FOUNTAIN OR A SNARE?

The teaching of the wise is a fountain of life, to turn aside from the snares of death.
Proverbs 13:14

The New Testament describes two young men who lived around the time when Jesus was on earth. Both of them knew that the Savior died on Calvary's cross. But that is where the similarity ends. Their names were Judas Iscariot, one of Jesus' original twelve disciples, and Timothy, a fellow missionary with the apostle Paul.

We don't know if Judas' parents loved God and were looking for the Messiah, or whether young Judas studied the Scriptures with his family. Matthew 10:4 records his name on the list of the twelve men who Jesus chose to be His closest followers, and John 6:71 tells us he was the son of Simon.

Timothy, on the other hand, is first introduced in Acts 16:1, where he is described as, "the son of a Jewish woman who was a believer, but his father was a Greek [and most likely an unbeliever]." Since Timothy was well spoken of by the other Christians in his home church, the apostle Paul asked him to join him on his missionary trip.

Judas appears to have had two major problems. Even though he spent great amounts of time with Jesus and the other disciples, he never trusted the Lord to be his personal Savior. And he was a greedy man. He probably agreed to join the group for what he could get out of it by way of money, miracles, and power.

Today's verse talks about people who refuse to obey God and therefore are caught in the "snare" or trap of spiritual death. Judas betrayed Jesus to the Jewish officials for the greedy gain of thirty pieces of silver. He had no peace or joy in this, and eventually he killed himself.

Timothy's mother and grandmother loved the Lord and taught him the Scriptures. Paul wrote, "For I am mindful of the sincere faith within you, which first dwelt in your grandmother Lois, and your mother Eunice, and I am sure that it is in you as well" (2 Timothy 1:5). The apostle saw the life of Christ bubbling up in this young man like a "fountain of life," and he wanted to help Timothy grow to be an even stronger servant of God.

The two young men, Judas Iscariot and Timothy, may have been somewhat similar in appearance, but were very different in nature and attitude. One ignored the Lord's kindness, betrayed our Savior, and took his own life in guilt and shame. The other was raised by a godly mother and grandmother, and became a great friend and fellow missionary with the apostle Paul.

Good Bible teaching is so important to a young person's development, isn't it? It can make the difference between a Judas and a Timothy.

WHAT DO YOU THINK?

1. Today's verse describes sin as a snare or trap. Which of Jesus' disciples fell into this snare and eventually took his own life?

2. What advantage did Timothy have over Judas Iscariot during his growing up years?

3. What does it mean that the teaching of wise people—like your parents—is a fountain of life?

ANSWERS TO YOUR QUESTIONS

1. *Judas Iscariot fell into the snare or trap of greed, so that he was willing to turn Jesus over to the priests for thirty pieces of silver.*

2. *The Bible doesn't really tell us anything about Judas' growing up years. However, we know from God's Word that Timothy's mother and grandmother were believers, they loved God, and taught him the Scriptures.*

3. *The teaching of wise people, if they are believers, can point young people to Christ. Then, as they learn to walk in obedience to their heavenly Father, the life of Jesus bubbles up in them like a fountain of life.*

43. WISE OR FOOLISH? WHICH WILL IT BE?

Every prudent man acts with knowledge, but a fool displays folly.
Proverbs 13:16

Did you know that all of us can be both "prudent" (wise) and "foolish" at different times in our lives? I can recall making foolish decisions, and I usually ended up paying for my lack of wisdom. I thank the Lord Jesus that I have also made some wise choices—usually with His help—with positive results for other people and me.

This is also true for Bible characters like Abraham, David, Moses, and even the apostles Paul and Peter. All made prudent and foolish choices. One of my favorite Old Testament prophets did too. His name was Elijah, and he lived in Gilead in the land of Israel. Because he obeyed God, the Lord used him to perform amazing miracles to show the disobedient nation of Israel the way back to God.

One day, God led Elijah to challenge 450 prophets of the supposed god Baal to a contest. Why? To show who the real God was—Jehovah, God of Israel, or their pagan god. This large group of phony prophets worked for Ahab, the evil king of Israel, and Queen Jezebel. Elijah and the prophets agreed to each build an altar, put a sacrificial ox on it, and then call on the name of their god. Elijah proclaimed, "The God who answers by fire, He is God" (1 Kings 18:24).

It's almost comical to read how the prophets of Baal danced around their altar; all their efforts amounted to a big fat zero. Elijah, on the other hand, poured gallons of water over his altar. When he called on the true God, "Then the fire of the Lord fell, and consumed the burnt offering and the wood and the stones and the dust, and licked up the water that was in the trench" (1 Kings 18:38). Wow! That's more exciting than any fireworks! It almost makes you want to stand up and cheer.

Then Queen Jezebel threatened to kill Elijah. Instead of talking to God about it, like he had before the contest with the prophets of Baal, he *ran away* into the wilderness. He forgot about God's great power—he thought only about the queen's murderous words. He became so tired and discouraged that he sat down under a juniper tree, "and he requested for himself that he might die, and said, 'It is enough; now, O Lord, take my life'" (1 Kings 19:4).

Could this really be the same Elijah that defeated the pagan prophets of Baal in front of the nation of Israel? Yes it is! During the contest with the phony prophets, he was confident in God's power to defeat evil. Unfortunately, he became so frightened by Jezebel's threats that he forgot God and his life went downhill from there. I'm so glad to read later on in the Bible that Elijah became a faithful spokesman for God once again.

WHAT DO YOU THINK?

1. After Elijah's great victory over the 450 prophets of Baal, what foolish decision did he make?

2. Do you think it's possible for all of us to make both wise decisions and foolish ones? Can you think of an example of each type that you have made in your life?

3. Is there any way that we can tip the balance in favor of making wise decisions over the foolish kind?

ANSWERS TO YOUR QUESTIONS

1. *When Queen Jezebel threatened to kill Elijah, he failed to ask God what he should do. Instead, he ran away and hid in the wilderness.*

2. *Personal opinion. You may want to ask each child.*

3. *I believe we will make more wise decisions than foolish ones if we ask God for His guidance and help. It's nice to know that we have God's promises in the Bible that He will make our way straight.*

44. WHEN TO SAVE AND WHEN TO SPEND

A good man leaves an inheritance to his children's children.
Proverbs 13:22

The Bible says a lot about how we should earn our money and also how we should spend it. The most important fact to remember is that everything we own—including ourselves—belongs to God. Psalm 24:1 says, "The earth is the Lord's, and all it contains, the world, and those who dwell in it." Since our money really belongs to God, don't you think we should consult Him regarding what we do with His funds?

Nobody wants to be called a *miser* or a *Scrooge,* which is someone who keeps his money just for himself and never thinks to be generous to others. God is so generous to us that we ought to be willing to help others who are in need.

I think it's important to have a plan when it comes to spending; here is one for young people to consider. Imagine you receive ten dollars each week as an allowance for doing jobs at home, cutting your neighbor's lawn, or baby sitting. As you get older (while still living at home), your expenses will increase, but let's say that until you are 16 years old, the 10-40-50 plan is a good one.

It means that you set aside ten percent of your money earned to *give back* to the Lord (10 percent of $10.00 would be $1.00). Since your parents pay for your food and clothing, your expenses will not be great, so you should be able to *save* forty percent of your earnings (40 percent of $10.00 would be $4.00). You could even put a little extra aside if there is something special like a summer mission trip that you want to save for. Finally, it's nice to have some money to *spend* and that could be fifty percent of your earnings. (50 percent of $10.00 would be $5.00.)

Of course, you don't have to spend the five dollars. There might be a missionary project at church; you could buy a gift for a needy child; or help a friend with a charity fundraiser. Just be sure to ask the Lord to help you to be wise in your spending, and He may even reward you one day in heaven for what you did with His money.

WHAT DO YOU THINK?

1. Since all our money and belongings really are God's, what should we do before we make any major decisions concerning these possessions?

2. Why save a set amount of our allowance each week instead of just spending it?

3. What is a good formula for handling your allowance or earnings until you're about 16 years of age when your expenses may increase?

ANSWERS TO YOUR QUESTIONS

1. *Since all our possessions really belong to God, we should ask Him to direct our thinking when it comes to how we spend our money.*

2. *Saving a set amount of our earnings every week is wise in case something special comes up that would cost more than your allowance that week.*

3. *A sensible plan for dealing with your weekly income until around 16 years of age is the "10-40-50 plan." That means 10% for the Lord's work; 40% for savings; and 50% for spending. NOTE TO PARENTS: The author recognizes that you as parents might be recommending some other course of action with your children regarding giving, saving, and spending. The intent here is to encourage discussion within the family on this important subject and not infer that there is only one plan.*

45. WHAT'S A ROD GOT TO DO WITH LOVE?

He who spares his rod hates his son, but he who loves him disciplines him diligently.
                                                    Proverbs 13:24

Do you know anyone who enjoys being disciplined for doing wrong? Deep down in our hearts we might know we deserve the punishment, but we still would rather avoid the pain or loss.

We've all seen a mother pushing her screaming child around a grocery store in a cart. Little four-year-old Debbie makes up her mind that she wants a Popsicle, *right now!* It's just not a convenient time for mom, so she promises to give Debbie any flavor she wants—at home. But Debbie doesn't feel she wants to wait, and so she begins to scream, knowing that if she yells loud enough and long enough, she may get what she wants. What do you think Debbie's mom should do?

Ronnie really wants to watch an NBA playoff game on TV. His dad asks him if he has finished his homework, and Ronnie says that he did it all at school. The next day the teacher sends a note home to the parents saying that Ronnie has not done his homework for the past two weeks. What should Ronnie's dad do?

Both children should be disciplined by their parents, shouldn't they? Debbie got angry because she couldn't have what she wanted when she wanted it. Ronnie lied to his father. Children who are never corrected by their parents, but are allowed to do or say whatever they want with no boundaries as far as right and wrong, become a shame to themselves and to their parents.

Today's verse says that when a child does something deserving of discipline, and the parent does not follow through, the mom or dad is failing to show him love. Why is that? By dealing with the child's wrong behavior, the parent is saying, "Ronnie or Debbie, you are my child—not someone else's—and because I love you like a father or mother, I take responsibility for you and your actions, just like God does with us."

The Lord told Israel, "Thus you are to know in your heart that the Lord your God was disciplining you just as a man disciplines his son. Therefore, you shall keep the commandments of the Lord your God, to walk in His ways and to fear Him" (Deuteronomy 8:5, 6). A child who is never rewarded for good behavior and corrected for wrong, never fully understands God's love or the true love of his parents.

I know it's a hard thing to do, but the next time mom and dad discipline you, try to remember that they really are showing parental love to you. It's important to them that you grow up to be a blessing to God, to others, and to yourself.

WHAT DO YOU THINK?

1. Does God discipline us because He is mad at us for sinning?

2. In what ways might God discipline us if we repeatedly disobey Him?

3. Please read Proverbs 29:15 and pick out two aspects of discipline. Do you remember what they are?

ANSWERS TO YOUR QUESTIONS

1. *God disciplines us for our good because He loves us. If He didn't love us, He would ignore us and not care what happened to us.*

2. *God has all kinds of ways to discipline us if we repeatedly disobey Him. He can use sickness, loss of money, loss of friends, failure at some goal—even embarrassment. He wants to lovingly get our attention so we will choose to obey Him.*

3. *The verse in Proverbs 29:15 mentions the rod (discipline) and reproof (clearly explaining why you are being disciplined.)*

46. WHEN COOL MEANS FOOL

Fools mock at sin, but among the upright there is good will [favor with God].
Proverbs 14:9

"Cool." Do you often use that word? I know that it's at least sixty years old, so it has lived a long time. Why's that? It's an easy expression to remember that describes what's popular among a group of people at any one time.

"Cool" stays alive, but the things it refers to—clothing and hairstyles, for example—constantly change. I'm sure during Bible times, young people knew which styles were popular and which ones were considered odd. Would you be cool if you wore those clothes to school now?

Who decides what clothes, hairdos, songs, activities, friends, or teachers are cool? Is there a catalog or website somewhere to help us find out? Or does everyone decide for herself? Maybe something could be cool in New York, but not cool in California.

Actually there is nothing necessarily wrong with wanting to wear clothes that are popular or to keep your hair in a current style—unless it looks freaky of course. Can you think of anything that would be wrong with wanting to look or be cool? I can think of at least one major reason.

Christians decide what is right and wrong by what the Bible teaches. God's Word has so much good information on how to dress, talk to people, and even choose our friends.

Unfortunately, a lot of the things that the majority of people decide is cool are just the opposite of God's Word. For example, in some schools, guys who are big, strong, and athletic are often called cool, while those with physical disabilities are not.

Is that how Jesus acted toward people He met on the roads of Judea? Did he only hang out with athletic guys and girls who had straight teeth and pretty hair? Remember Zaccheus? In Luke 19:3 we read that he was a hated tax gatherer and was "small in stature." He definitely was not cool. But, it's interesting that out of that whole crowd of people, Jesus chose to stay at Zaccheus' house.

Today's verse says that fools mock at sin. Sometimes, people who would rather be cool than obey God treat sin the same way. On the other hand, those who choose God's Word over what is currently popular, receive favor from God. Now that sounds cool to me!

WHAT DO YOU THINK?

1. Who decides what is "cool" as far as clothes, hair styles, and entertainers?

2. Usually there is a group at school that decides what things are cool and what are not. If we don't make our own decisions, what dangers are we stepping into?

3. How does doing what is considered cool by the group at school often line up with God's direction in His Word? On what basis did Jesus make His decisions when He was on earth?

ANSWERS TO YOUR QUESTIONS

1. *There is no one person or group that decides what clothes, hair styles, music, or even attitudes are cool. It differs with age groups and location in the country. What is considered cool definitely changes between generations. Technology like the internet and wireless telephones pass such information on styles and preferences around the globe so much faster now.*

2. *If someone else is deciding for Christian young people what is popular and cool, there is a very good chance it will not line up with what the Bible says. Then, the Christian young person has to decide if he wants to please the world or please God. Some choices like clothes and hair styles would be considered "neutral" since God does not discuss them in Scripture, except for the exhortation to dress modestly.*

3. *All Christians' decisions and choices ought to be measured against God's Word. Everything that is called cool isn't necessarily contrary to the Bible. However, when it is, we need to follow what God has said. When Jesus was on earth, He did only what His Father told Him.*

47. I LIKE MY WAY—EVEN IF IT'S WRONG

There is a way which seems right to a man, but its end is the way of death.

Proverbs 14:12

I enjoy talking with strangers on airplanes—especially about the Lord. I've sat next to quite a variety of people over the years. Some obviously don't want to talk, and as soon as they fasten their seat belts, they put on their headphones and disappear into their own little worlds. I haven't had enough nerve yet to pick up one of their earphones and say, "Hey, guy! How would you like to talk? I'm a pretty interesting person, and I've got some great stories."

Other people will put their heads back, close their eyes, and go into hibernation until the wheels of the plane touch down. I've thought of prying open one of their eyes and asking, "Is there anyone home in there?" But I always reject that idea too.

Once in a while a businessman will half-heartedly flip through a magazine, and I'll start asking him a few innocent questions like, "Are you travelling on business or pleasure?" or, "In what part of the country do you live?"

Before long I will often say, "Can I ask you a question?" They usually agree, so I'll say, "If our plane should suddenly crash, all of us would be dead. If you found yourself standing before God and He asked you, 'Why should I, who am perfectly holy, allow you into my holy heaven,' what would you say to Him"?

Most people give me a similar answer. A businessman might say, "I've been a good father to my kids. I love my wife. I go to church every Sunday. I think I'm a pretty good person. I think God will weigh up my good deeds against my bad actions, and there will be more good than bad. Then He will let me into heaven."

At that point, I share a few verses from the Bible that clearly show that we cannot be saved by our good deeds, but only by believing that Christ died on the cross to pay for our sins.

Unfortunately, people will often ignore what the Bible says and reply, "Well, I think I'll take my chances." How very sad that people choose to set aside God's very own words in favor of their own way. And man's way, according to Solomon, ends in death!

WHAT DO YOU THINK?

1. Think of a good question to ask a person—whether on a plane or anywhere that seems to be appropriate—to get them to think about heaven and eternity. [Note: You may want to have each child contribute to a group answer; you could even role play.]

2. Imagine a friend tells you they'll take a chance on getting to heaven because they've done more good things than bad. How could you help them see the truth of God's one way to heaven?

3. Since our good works cannot qualify us to go to heaven when we die, what will qualify us?

ANSWERS TO YOUR QUESTIONS

1. *What would you say to God if you died today, suddenly found yourself standing before Him, and He asked you, "Why should I, who am holy, allow you into My perfect heaven"?*

2. *I would ask him or her if I could share what God actually says about it—and since He is the One with whom we have to deal, His words are most important. (Romans 3:23; Ephesians 2:8, 9; Titus 3:5)*

3. *The only thing that will qualify us to go to heaven when we die is that we have believed or trusted in the gospel of Jesus Christ. According to 1 Corinthians 15:1-4, the gospel is that Jesus died for our sins, that He was buried, and that He arose from the dead on the third day.*

48. SLIDING BACKWARDS INTO UNHAPPINESS

The backslider in heart will have his fill of his own ways, but a good man [or woman] will be satisfied with his.
Proverbs 14:14

Do you know anyone who would rather be totally unhappy and discouraged with his life than be happy and satisfied? I'm guessing that most people want to live a meaningful life and make a positive difference in the world.

The Bible is our textbook where God shows us how to live life to the full and be content. The choices we make are key. I have known a lot of unbelievers who are miserable with how their lives turned out—their job, their family, and even their friends. And I'm sorry to say that I know some Christians who are also hard to be around, because they constantly grumble.

Today's verse talks about a "backslider." This is a Christian who chooses not to confess his sin to God. At some point, he has decided that no one is going to tell him what to do—including the Lord. He is still saved, but he is disobedient and has *slidden backwards into sin.* Our verse says that such a person is not happy, even though he is his own boss.

I am embarrassed to say that I did this as a young Christian man in college. I chose to walk in sin, rather than obey my heavenly Father. I was just like the backslider—I was miserable! I didn't find joy or contentment by walking in sin. Just like today's verse says, I had my fill of having my own way.

God could have disciplined me severely for my disobedience, but instead He kindly and lovingly brought me back into fellowship with Himself. And He used my wife to draw me; she had just come to know Jesus as her Savior. I confessed my sin to my heavenly Father and once again began to enjoy my life with Him.

From that point on, I can honestly say I love my life and the blessings God has showered on my family. The Lord gave me a godly wife, three dear children with spouses who love Jesus, and almost a dozen precious grandchildren. I'm convinced that a Christian who obeys God will be satisfied with her life, while someone who slides backwards into sin will be pretty unhappy with hers.

WHAT DO YOU THINK?

1. What does it mean for a Christian to be a "backslider?" Can *unbelievers* be backsliders?

2. As a born again Christian, how can we experience maximum joy and fulfillment?

3. Please explain in your own words what today's verse means when it says that a Christian who is a backslider in heart will "have his fill of his own ways."

ANSWERS TO YOUR QUESTIONS

1. *A backslider is a Christian who chooses to live in sin and not confess that sin to God. They are still saved, but they are disobedient and have slidden backwards into sin. Unbelievers have never been born again and forgiven of their sins by God, so they cannot be Christian backsliders.*

2. *Christians can only experience maximum joy and fulfillment when they walk under the control of the Holy Spirit who lives inside them. The Holy Spirit will always lead Christians in ways that agree with the Bible.*

3. *Personal opinion. You may want to ask each child.*

49. WHAT'S WRONG WITH GETTING ANGRY?

He who is slow to anger has great understanding, but he who is quick-tempered exalts folly [increases foolishness].
Proverbs 14:29

Why did God get angry at the disobedient nation of Israel in the wilderness, and yet His Word tells us that we should not get angry? We read, "For they [Israel] have rejected the law of the Lord of hosts…On this account the anger of the Lord has burned against His people" (Isaiah 5:24b, 25a). But in Ephesians 4:31 it says, "Let all bitterness and wrath and anger …be put away from you."

There must be a type of anger that is wrong, since there are so many verses in Proverbs that warn us against it—like Proverbs 15:18, 16:32, and 19:11. Today's verse talks about an angry person we often see—someone who is quick-tempered or easily "flies off the handle."

You've probably seen two boys at a playground or on the street start out by saying unkind words to each other, and pretty soon they are wrestling on the ground.

So, what is the difference between God being angry and people losing their tempers? Ephesians 4:26 gives us help with this: "Be angry, and yet do not sin; do not let the sun go down on your anger." God made our bodies and our minds, and He gave us emotions and feelings to more fully enjoy Him and the world around us. Jesus expressed many emotions when He interacted with people—and we were created in God's image. That means we can experience joy, peace, friendship, and excitement. And we can also feel upset or disturbed, usually by something another person does or says to us.

The key here is that although God wants us to have emotions, He also wants us to be under His control all the time. He doesn't want us to react so strongly that we do and say things that are actually sinful. What He means in Ephesians 4:26 is, "If you are going to be angry, let me control you and help you not to react so strongly that you sin."

We know that God is perfectly holy; He has never sinned and never will. Our heavenly Father did get angry at times, especially when Israel refused to obey His Word and worshipped pagan idols. However, He never lost control of His holiness. He is slow to anger (Psalm 103:8).

I'm so thankful that every time my emotions react strongly, I can immediately ask the Lord to keep me under His control.

WHAT DO YOU THINK?

1. What is the difference between the way we often get angry and God's anger against sin?

2. In Genesis 4:5 and 8 we read, "So Cain became very angry and his countenance [face] fell [looked sad and depressed]... And Cain told Abel his brother. And it came about when they were in the field, that Cain rose up against Abel his brother and killed him." What do you think about Cain's anger problem?

3. Are you and I capable of seriously hurting someone if we get angry enough? Is it possible for Christians to be angry and not sin?

ANSWERS TO YOUR QUESTIONS

1. *Very often when we get angry, we lose control—that is, we stop being controlled by the Lord and we sin. We say hurtful, critical things about other people, and we end up damaging friendships. When God gets angry, He never sins and is always under the control of His holiness and perfection. We can get angry over all kinds of things, but God gets angry at sin.*

2. *Cain was most likely jealous of his brother Abel, because God blessed Abel's sacrifice and rejected Cain's. Jealousy is sin, and because Cain did not confess his sin to God and receive forgiveness, it continued to build up, until, like a volcano, it spilled over into a white-hot rage, and he killed his own brother.*

3. *Personal opinion. You may want to ask each child. I believe we are all capable of getting angry enough at someone else that we could hurt them. We seem to lose all control and common sense when we get very angry. If we keep walking with the Lord Jesus by faith under His control, we can be angry and not sin. When we obey the Lord, even when our emotions are stirred up, He will often still use us for His purposes.*

50. IS AMERICA A CHRISTIAN COUNTRY?

Righteousness exalts a nation, but sin is a disgrace to any people.
Proverbs 14:34

Is America a Christian country? It appears that our first president, George Washington, honored God, believed in Jesus Christ, and respected His Word. A historian wrote, "On the very first national Thanksgiving under the Constitution, Washington said, 'It is the duty of all nations to acknowledge the providence [kindness and care] of Almighty God, to obey His will, to be grateful for His benefits, and humbly to implore His protection and favor.' He spoke of Christ as 'the divine Author of our blessed religion.' He encouraged missionaries who were seeking to 'Christianize the aboriginals.' He wrote of 'the blessed religion revealed in the Word of God.' He encouraged seekers to learn 'the religion of Jesus Christ.'"

Back in 1831, a man named Samuel Francis Smith wrote the stirring song called simply "America." Verse 4 reads like this: "Our father's God to Thee, author of liberty, to Thee we sing. Long may our land be bright, with freedom's holy light, protect us by Thy might, Great God our King." Although this music is almost 200 years old, it is still sung at important American events.

Because the USA is a democratic republic, there is freedom of speech and of worship—there is even freedom to believe in no religion. Therefore our government doesn't make anyone follow any one religion.

It would be wonderful to say that the United States of America is a truly Christian country, but unfortunately that is questionable. Millions of citizens call themselves "Christians," but many other religions are represented here as well. We can at least say that our great country was *founded* on Christian principles, and Bible truths were used as a framework for our laws and society.

Written in 1782, one of the earliest declarations concerning the day of Thanksgiving read: "The United States in Congress assembled, taking into their consideration the many instances of divine goodness to these States...Do hereby recommend to the inhabitants of these States in general, the observation of Thursday the 28th day of November next, as a day of solemn thanksgiving to God for all His mercies: and they do further recommend to all ranks, to testify to their gratitude to God for His goodness, by a cheerful obedience of His laws, and by promoting, each in his station, and by his influence, the practice of true and undefiled religion, which is the great foundation of public prosperity and national happiness."

Whether or not America is a truly Christian country, one thing we know for sure is that God has blessed us in more ways than we can even count.

WHAT DO YOU THINK?

1. Who was America's first president? What do we know about his beliefs, based on things he said and wrote?

2. What document was frequently used by our Founding Fathers as a moral standard or framework for America's laws and system of justice?

3. There are some people who feel strongly that God raised up the USA to be a Christian light to the rest of the world and an example of what God could also do for them? What are your thoughts about this?

ANSWERS TO YOUR QUESTIONS

1. *America's first president was George Washington, and it appears that he honored God, believed in Jesus Christ, and respected the Bible. He even was very positive toward reaching the North American Indians with the gospel.*

2. *God's precious Word, the Bible, was used by our country's founding fathers to develop a framework or structure for our country's laws and justice system.*

3. *Personal opinion. The various children could add on information to form a group answer.*

51. A SOFT ANSWER—NOT A HARSH REPLY

A gentle answer turns away wrath, but a harsh word stirs up anger.

Proverbs 15:1

Have you ever seen *one* person angrily discussing two sides of an issue? Probably not, since it takes at least two people to have an argument.

So, as Christians, what should we do when someone lashes out at us with harsh words? Should we just act like a zombie, stare straight ahead, and say nothing? That might infuriate the other person even more.

Today's verse advises us to give a *gentle* answer. When an angry person receives a kind but honest response, they find it hard to keep up their emotional outburst. Instead, they lower their voice and become less passionate with their comments.

There is a dramatic example of this principle in 2 Samuel 16. Absalom, a son of King David, revolts against his father in order to become the king himself. He wins over the majority of the Jewish people to his side, forcing his father to flee from Jerusalem with a few friends.

As the little group escapes from the city, Shimei, a relative of the former King Saul, begins to curse and throw stones at David and his few friends, saying, "Get out, get out, you man of bloodshed, and worthless fellow. The Lord has returned upon you all the bloodshed of the house of Saul, in whose place you have reigned; and the Lord has given the kingdom into the hand of your son Absalom. And behold, you are taken in your own evil, for you are a man of bloodshed" (2 Samuel 16:7, 8). Even though Shimei mentions God in his abusive rants, it doesn't mean that he honors God or does His will.

As you would expect, David's loyal bodyguards want to punish Shimei for his disrespect. Abishai says, "Why should this dead dog curse my lord the king? Let me go over now, and cut off his head" (2 Samuel 16:9).

Does David then tell Abishai to go and teach Shimei a permanent lesson? No! The king says, "If he curses, and if the

Lord has told him, 'Curse David,' then who shall say, 'Why have you done so?'" Later, David says, "Let him alone and let him curse, for the Lord has told him" (verse 11).

Wow! What a man of grace David was! What a tremendous example of giving a soft answer in response to harsh criticism! David obviously chose to let his heavenly Father deal with Shimei's anger.

Do you suppose we would get similar results if we gave a gentle answer in response to angry remarks someone makes to us? Let's prove God's promise to be true. His Word says that a gentle answer will turn away anger.

WHAT DO YOU THINK?

1. Explain in your own words, what David's situation was in today's story, and what took place as he fled from Jerusalem.

2. What kind of response would you expect from a king toward someone cursing and throwing stones at him?

3. Why do you think David was able to show such humility and grace to Shimei, and give him a "soft answer"?

ANSWERS TO YOUR QUESTIONS

1. *David's son Absalom rebelled against his father, turned the people of Israel against him, and took over his throne. As David and his few loyal friends escaped from Jerusalem, Shimei, a relative of the previous King Saul, saw David's group and began to heap accusations on him of all the people he had killed. He even threw stones at him.*

2. *You would expect a king to order his bodyguards to immediately go to Shimei and kill him.*

3. *David was a man after God's own heart—in other words, at this point in his life, he lived to do God's will. He interpreted Shimei's abuse as an action that God allowed, and that he probably needed.*

52. IS GOD REALLY EVERYWHERE?

The eyes of the Lord are in every place, watching the evil and the good.
Proverbs 15:3

It's hard for us to grasp the fact that God is everywhere in the universe at the same time. No one can say, "Sorry, God was just here, but He left. You just missed Him!"

The Psalmist David was just as amazed at God's *everywhere presence* as we are. He wrote, "Where can I go from [Your] Spirit? Or where can I flee from [Your] presence? If I take the wings of the dawn, if I dwell in the remotest part of the sea, even there [Your] hand will lead me, and [Your] right hand will lay hold of me" (Psalm 139:7, 9, 10).

Not only is God everywhere at the same time—including everywhere we are—but He sees just as well in the dark as at noon. Criminals usually do their dirty work at night thinking that no one will see them. David wrote, "Even the darkness is not dark to [You], and the night is as bright as the day. Darkness and light are alike to [You]" (Psalm 139:12).

What about you? Is it easier to give in to temptation when there is no one around who knows you—or if you are by yourself—than when you are with family and friends? I find temptation to be very strong at those times. After all, who is going to know about our sin that really matters? God will—and He is the most important One of all.

Did you know also, that since God is everywhere all the time, that He was there in your mother's womb when you were first formed? Listen as the creator God describes the scene through His servant David: "My frame [body] was not hidden from [You], when I was made in secret, and skillfully wrought in the depths of the earth [my mother's womb]. [Your] eyes have seen my unformed substance; and in [Your] book they were all written, the days that were ordained for me, when as yet there was not one of them" (Psalm 139:15, 16).

Isn't that thrilling? God was able to watch when you were just a few tiny cells coming together. If you could have miraculously looked at yourself under a microscope when you were just one or two days old, you would have seen a clump of several cells that wouldn't even look like a body. And then our heavenly Father watched as each clump of cells began to take on a shape more like a body. I imagine He rejoiced as the cells that formed your heart began to pulsate for the first time. God was not just a silent spectator, but He gave life to us—directly from His heart of love.

What are your thoughts after hearing that God is everywhere all the time? God is not watching in order to catch you doing something wrong. If you are His child, He loves you more than you can even imagine. He is always close to you to help and protect you. After all, Jesus died for you so you could live forever with Him in heaven. How wonderful that the God of the universe loves you and me all the time, wherever we are!

WHAT DO YOU THINK?

1. How is it possible for God to see when there isn't a single light anywhere near?

2. When you are with a group of friends and you are tempted to do something your parents would not want you to do, do you ever think about the fact that the Lord Jesus is right there next to you? How does it affect your decision?

3. If God is there in our mother's womb when we are first formed, and participates in our development, when do we actually become a person—right then, or when we are born into the world?

ANSWERS TO YOUR QUESTIONS

1. *One of God's characteristics is that He is all-powerful. That means that NOTHING is too difficult for Him—He can do anything He desires to do, including seeing in the dark.*

2. *Personal opinion. You may want to ask each child this question.*

3. *We become a unique person when we are first formed as a shapeless clump of cells—also called "conception." Since God is everywhere, He was also there in your mother's womb when this miracle of life occurred (See Psalm 139:15, 16).*

53. HOW TO PLEASE GOD IN ONE EASY STEP

The sacrifice of the wicked is an abomination to the Lord, but the prayer of the upright is His delight.
Proverbs 15:8

"You are in our thoughts and prayers." TV anchors and news people often say that when they report on a tragic accident. I have no idea whether they actually pray, or whether it's just their way of saying, "I feel bad about what you are going through." In other words, it's become popular to talk about praying for people without any real plan to do so.

Today's verse gives us a clue about how to delight God's heart—and who wouldn't want to do that? If we are believers in Jesus Christ, then we have God's promise that it brings Him great joy when we choose to talk with Him.

There are thousands of books on the topic of how and when to pray. But I don't think it's that complicated. Here are a few thoughts on this very important area of the Christian life:

1. Prayer is primarily about God and not about us. Like everything else in our walk with Him, prayer is all about our Savior's pleasure and His glory. It's easy to focus on what we will get from God if we pray, instead of talking with Him about what He desires.

2. Prayer is an amazing privilege. Just think about it—the Creator of the entire universe allows us to talk with Him whenever we want to and for as long as we want. Try doing that with the President of the United States!

3. What is *not* a part of real prayer? Saying the same words over and over like a ritual; using flowery words to try to impress those who hear us and maybe even God; giving information to those with whom we're praying; or preaching a mini-sermon—these all have no place in prayer. And it's definitely not something we have to do to keep God from getting angry at us.

4. Prayer is not an event that only takes place before meals, before we go to sleep, or at certain planned times at church. It's an attitude of mind that begins when we first wake up,

125

and continues until we fall asleep at night. Yes, I still have special times when I pray through my list of requests, separated by times of praise and worship. But more and more I find myself discussing with God something that I just saw or did, like you would do with a special friend standing right beside you—because He is. So, prayer is becoming less and less a specific time where I bow my head, close my eyes, and have a "time of prayer," and more and more an unending conversation with God as I go about my daily life.

WHAT DO YOU THINK?

1. What does God say delights His heart? What group of people is He talking about?

2. Which posture or position does God prefer we take when we pray? Does He prefer that we stand, kneel or sit?

3. If prayer is *not* about what we get out of it, or a way for us to "make points" with God, what *is* prayer about?

ANSWERS TO YOUR QUESTIONS

1. *According to today's verse, the prayer of the upright or the Christian delights God's heart. He loves to hear from us at any time of the night or day, for as long as we want.*

2. *God is more concerned with our attitude of heart when we pray, than what position we're in.*

3. *Prayer is primarily about what pleases God and His glory, rather than what we like and what we get out of it.*

54. WHY BE A MOPER WHEN YOU CAN BE A CHEERER-UPPER?

All the days of the afflicted are bad, but a cheerful heart has a continual feast.

Proverbs 15:15

One of the most interesting characters in the popular Winnie-the-Pooh series has to be Eeyore. You remember him—he's the stuffed donkey who sees the whole world through "blue glasses." We could call him a *moper* because he constantly mopes or complains about how difficult his life is—something negative is sure to happen. Time and again, Eeyore loses his tail and is heard to say, "It's not much of a tail, but I'm sort of attached to it."[2]

Believe it or not, there are people like Eeyore—not because they lose a tail, but because they tend to see the negative side of everything. They are sure something terrible is going to happen, even on a happy occasion. If you bring it to their attention they will likely say, "I'm just being realistic."

Today's verse talks about the benefit of a cheerful heart. We really do have a choice in how we look at our world. There are plenty of negative things happening all the time, and if we choose to focus on them, we can easily become depressed. There are other Eeyores who look more at the future than the present, and predict that the light at the end of the tunnel is probably a train.

Psalm 37:23 says, "The steps of a man are established [determined] by the Lord." This means that God is in control of a Christian's life, and nothing negative will happen without the Lord's loving permission. He also promises in Hebrews 13:5 to never desert us or forsake us. That should be reason enough to celebrate every single day.

Caleb is one of my Old Testament heroes who kept a positive outlook. He was an amazing man of Israel who lived about 1500 years before Christ came to earth. Before the Israelites left the wilderness, God told Moses to send twelve spies into the Promised Land of Canaan to look it over. Caleb was one of the twelve along with his friend Joshua, who became Israel's leader after Moses died. God already knew that Canaan was a land that flowed with milk and honey. He also knew that He was prepared to defeat Israel's enemies, but He wanted Israel to turn to Him and trust Him.

After a forty day search in Canaan, the twelve returned with different reports. Caleb told Moses, "We should by all means go up and take possession of it, for we shall surely overcome it" (Numbers 13:30). Joshua agreed with him. Clearly these two men trusted the Lord. The other ten spies could only think of themselves, instead of what God is able to do. They said, "We are not able to go up against the people, for they are too strong for us." Doesn't that sound vaguely like Eeyore?

Caleb chose to be cheerful and positive all his life. Not only did his attitude create a continual feast of joy and fellowship with God, but a banquet of blessing for those who knew him.

WHAT DO YOU THINK?

1. True or False - We have the choice to make whether we are going to be grumpy and negative (like Eeyore) or cheerful and positive (like Caleb).

2. Why was the Canaan report of Caleb and Joshua so different from that of the other ten spies? What did the two understand that the others did not?

3. Psalm 37:23 says, "The steps of a man are _____by the Lord." What is the missing word and what does the verse mean?

ANSWERS TO YOUR QUESTIONS

1. *True! Our attitude is a choice we make.*

2. *Caleb and Joshua knew that God was all-powerful, and that He loved the nation of Israel. God had already promised He would defeat Israel's enemies if His people would just trust His Word. Caleb and Joshua trusted God and His promises.*

3. *The steps of a man are "established" [planned out] by the Lord. This verse means that God knows all about our lives— and since we all belong to Him, He decides when our lives will end. Everything that affects us has to first pass through His hands before it reaches us. Now that's a great reason to be cheerful!*

55. PROUD, PROUDER, AND PROUDEST

Pride goes before destruction, and a haughty spirit before stumbling. It is better to be of a humble spirit with the lowly, than to divide the spoil with the proud.
Proverbs 16:18, 19

Adam and Eve disobeyed God—all people inherited their sin of pride, including you and me. Pride is more obvious in some people than others, but all pride is sin.

In professional sports, for example, pride stands out in living color. Watch a football player run for a one yard touchdown. It's often followed by lots of chest pounding, prancing around, and pointing at self. The rest of the team may have slugged it out for eighty yards, but one guy feels free to take credit for the six points. Not much humility there.

Now and then an athlete (usually a Christian) demonstrates gentleness and patience. Just because they aren't yelling and throwing their hat on the ground, it doesn't mean they aren't tough and competitive.

When I think of humility in sports, I think of Tony Dungy, an outspoken Christian and former coach of the Indianapolis Colts—a Super Bowl winner. When asked if he ever raised his voice at his players, Tony said, "Only once!"—when a player failed to show up for a charitable event.

What is the lesson here? Isn't it that *true* success and riches are the products of being humble, rather than of being arrogant and proud? The main reason is because humility is part of the character of Christ. Matthew 11:29 is one of the few verses where Jesus describes Himself. He said, "Take My yoke upon you, and learn from Me, for I am gentle and humble in heart."

Christian growth is all about becoming more like Jesus. Pride should have no place in our lives—it will only hold us back from becoming a more mature Christian. Besides that, today's verses say that pride will eventually lead to destruction—of our family, our friends, our job, and anything else of value in our lives.

Since my main goal in life is to please my heavenly Father, I'm going to ask Him for strength to be humble. How about you?

WHAT DO YOU THINK?

1. What's wrong with being proud and telling people how great you are?

2. How do you think a professional coach like Tony Dungy was able to maintain a calm and patient attitude with all the pressure on him?

3. What is the difference between an athlete boasting about how talented he is and a parent who is proud of how well their child played the piano at a concert?

ANSWERS TO YOUR QUESTIONS

1. *Boasting and being proud is what Satan is like. Jesus described Himself as being gentle and humble in heart—and He wants us to be like Him.*

2. *Tony Dungy is probably aware that he is just like everyone else, and could easily have gotten loud and angry like so many other coaches. He is probably also aware of his testimony as a Christian, and was depending on the Lord to help him be the best he could be.*

3. *There probably are a lot of differences, but one main one is that the parent is happy for someone else's accomplishment and success. The athlete who pounds his chest and brags about how great he is, is only concerned with himself. And that can be ugly!*

56. TRUSTING GOD WHEN THE HEAT IS ON

He who gives attention to the word shall find good, and blessed is he who trusts in the Lord.
Proverbs 16:20

You can find a lot of *superheroes* in the exciting stories of the Bible, but they weren't made of plastic—they were actual flesh and blood. Daniel, Shadrach, Meshach, and Abednego are four young men who are special heroes of mine.

They were probably teenagers when they were kidnapped along with many other Hebrew residents of Jerusalem and forced to go to Babylon. It happened about 600 years before Jesus came to earth. The teens loved God and faced great challenges to their faith in this strange new country.

Nebuchadnezzar, king of Babylon, was so proud that he had a ninety-foot, golden statue made of himself. Then each day, when a certain signal was given, he required everyone to bow down and worship his image. There were serious consequences if anyone refused: "But whoever does not fall down and worship shall immediately be cast into the midst of a furnace of blazing fire" (Daniel 3:6).

The young Hebrew men worshipped the living God of Israel, so they would not bow down to the king's statue. Some evil men reported this act of defiance to Nebuchadnezzar, who had Shadrach, Meshach, and Abednego brought to him. Once again the king orders the three teens to bow down and worship his statue or be thrown into the furnace.

I love the young men's answer! "Shadrach, Meshach and Abednego answered and said to the king, 'O Nebuchadnezzar, we do not need to give you answer concerning this matter. If it be so, our God whom we serve is able to deliver us from the furnace of blazing fire; and He will deliver us out of your hand, O king. But even if He does not, let it be known to you, O king, that we are not going to serve your gods or worship the golden image that you have set up'" (Daniel 3:16-18).

Wow! Isn't that fantastic? They are true superheroes! They were respectful to the king, but they made it very clear that they would only worship the one and only true God.

You and I will never have to face a choice quite like the three Hebrew teens. But there will be tests. For example:

1. You are with a group of young people when someone makes an insulting remark about Jesus or Christianity. Will you trust the Lord and speak up in His defense? It's not a furnace, but it is a test of your willingness to trust God and stand up for Him.

2. One of your friends may suggest that you both do something that you are sure neither your parents nor the Lord would want. Can you trust the Lord and say "No"?

Just remember today's verse—"Blessed is he [or she] who trusts in the Lord."

WHAT DO YOU THINK?

1. What does biblical or Christian courage mean?

2. Would there have been anything wrong with the three young men just bowing down and pretending to worship the statue, but in their own hearts still worship the true God?

3. Can you think of any examples other than the two mentioned, where you might be called on to be courageous and trust God with a decision, rather than go along with what is popular in the world?

ANSWERS TO YOUR QUESTIONS

1. *Christian courage means to do what is right and in agreement with the Bible, regardless of the cost.*

2. *That would have been compromise and dishonesty. They would be looking like they were worshipping a pagan king to those around them, while at the same time trying to worship God on the inside. True worship involves both the inside (our hearts) and the outside (our testimony).*

3. *Personal opinion. You may want to ask each child.*

57. THE GOSSIP TEST

*A worthless man digs up evil, while his words are as a scorching
fire. A perverse [wicked] man spreads strife, and a slanderer
[gossiper] separates intimate friends.*
                    Proverbs 16:27, 28

Gossip can kill friendships! God describes people who
regularly gossip as worthless and perverse; they purposely try to
hurt others.

I'm sure I have gossiped at times, and it has hurt my friends
and displeased my heavenly Father. Wouldn't it be good if there
was a test we could use to check out all the things we say about
people? Here are five questions to ask ourselves *before* we share
information about someone who's not present—we'll call it a
"gossip test."

1. **Am I sharing this information to look like I know a lot
   about what's happening?** We can gossip at times to brag
   about how well-informed we are. We're probably not even
   thinking about the person we are gossiping about. This often
   happens when we are in a group of people that is criticizing
   others who aren't there. When there's an opening, we jump in
   and share our juicy little morsel of information. To make it
   worse, we could even make up some details to spice up the
   story.

2. **Am I purposely trying to hurt a person by speaking
   negatively about them to others?** Imagine that someone has
   done something or said something that hurt you. You should
   go and talk with that person privately. However, you may feel
   it's easier to spread untrue stories about them. This is sure to
   complicate your whole relationship with your friend and hurt
   your walk with Jesus.

3. **Was this information shared with me in confidence; did I
   agree to keep it private?** It's easy to agree to keep
   information to yourself. It's also easy to convince yourself
   that it won't hurt to tell just one other person. If you do,
   you're breaking your word, and it could easily qualify as
   gossip.

4. **Did it come to mind to pray for that person instead of sharing negative information?** I believe the Holy Spirit puts a check in our mind just before we gossip—it's like a stop sign. Wouldn't it be great to stop and silently pray for that person, instead of saying negative things about them? That would be a true friend, wouldn't it?

5. **Would I feel free to pass on this negative information if Jesus was standing next to me?** The truth is, Jesus is standing next to us. If we are a Christian, He lives inside us through the Holy Spirit. What a difference that would make to all of our conversations if we were aware of that one fact.

So, what do you think? Could the *gossip test* help you when you're not sure whether to share information about people with others?

WHAT DO YOU THINK?

1. To what does God compare gossip that is "hot" and "harmful"?

2. Try describing a possible situation where gossip is just an opportunity for someone to brag on herself?

3. Please read Proverbs 20:19 and explain the verse in your own words.

ANSWERS TO YOUR QUESTIONS

1. *God compares gossip to a scorching fire.*

2. *Personal opinion. You may want to ask each child. A young girl is at a ninth grade sleepover. Just after the lights go out for the night, the conversation turns to girls that either didn't come or weren't invited. In order to contribute to the criticism, she chimes in with negative comments about someone—and to impress the other girls more, she adds a few details that never happened. Today's verses say that her words are perverse or wicked, and that she separates friends.*

3. *In Proverbs 20:19, God tells us not to associate or be friends with a person who regularly gossips. Unless we want our own name dragged down, we should obey His counsel.*

58. CHILDREN, FATHERS, AND GRANDDADS

Grandchildren are the crown of old men, and the glory of sons is their fathers.

Proverbs 17:6

Today's verse describes three generations of a family— children, fathers, and grandfathers. The relationships between these three groups are important to God, and should be to us. As a young person, you probably don't think too often about the role your father and grandfather play in the forming of your personality.

God says that grandchildren are the "crown" of old men. That means that when grandchildren grow up and become loving servants of God, it shows what a positive influence the grandparents had on their lives.

A *grandfather* can concentrate on important things with his grandchildren like: going out for a Saturday morning, all-you-can-eat breakfast; shooting free throws in the driveway hoop; and taking in the circus where you taste-test each of the junk foods available.

A *father* can watch his daughter score her first goal in soccer and enjoy it more than the Super Bowl.

A *son or daughter* can copy some of their granddad's facial expressions and old fashioned words, because they respect him so much.

Surprisingly, the Bible doesn't talk much about these three generations of people in the same story. One exception is a family whose history occupies 38 chapters of Scripture. Do you know their names? Yes, it's Abraham, Isaac, and Jacob.

God promised Abraham and Sarah a son; Isaac was miraculously born when his father was one hundred years old. Many generations later, the Savior of the world, Jesus Christ, was born from that son's family. Isaac married Rebekah and they had two sons, Esau and Jacob. When Jacob grew up, he was the father of twelve sons who became the twelve tribes of Israel.

Isn't it wonderful how God worked through a grandfather, a father, and a son, to bring us our Savior?

WHAT DO YOU THINK?

1. Which family of three generations do we read a lot about in the Old Testament book of Genesis?

2. How old was Abraham when God finally gave him and his wife Sarah a son?

3. What does it mean that "grandchildren are the crown of old men"?

ANSWERS TO YOUR QUESTIONS

1. *Abraham, Isaac and Jacob (Israel),*

2. *Abraham was 100 years old when God gave his wife and him a son—they called him Isaac.*

3. *Grandfathers (and grandmothers) have a special love for their grandchildren. Also, when grandchildren become godly adults and servants of God, it speaks of the positive impact the grandparents' lives had on the family.*

59. MY BROTHER, MY FRIEND

A friend loves at all times, and a brother [or sister] is born for adversity.

Proverbs 17:17

When you stop and think, it's really a good thing to have one or more brothers or sisters. It means that while you are growing up, you always have someone close to your age with whom you can do fun things.

Unfortunately, people are usually adults before they fully realize what a good thing they had. Although I had no brothers, I was fortunate to have a sister, even though she was four years older than me. We are still good friends.

It troubles me when brothers and sisters say hurtful things to each other. Clearly they don't value one another like they should. And the insults can leave wounds that continue into their adult years.

Here are some biblical examples. When King David of Israel was a boy, he brought food from home to his brothers serving at the front lines of the army. Eliab, David's oldest brother, said, "Why have you come down? And with whom have you left those few sheep in the wilderness? I know your insolence [lack of respect] and the wickedness of your heart; for you have come down in order to see the battle" (1 Samuel 17:28).

Ouch! What an ungrateful guy Eliab was! Instead of thanking David for his kindness, he cut his younger brother down.

In contrast, there is David and Jonathan. Although not related, they were brothers in the Lord and deeply loved God.

In the New Testament, we read about Andrew who got so excited when he first met Jesus—the long-awaited Messiah—that he went right away to find his brother, Simon, so he could share in the joy (John 1:41). The disciples James and John also seemed to be very close, not only as brothers, but also as friends.

Then there's the apostle Paul who was older than Timothy, but he treated the younger man like a brother. He encouraged him and taught him how to be a witness for Jesus Christ.

"A brother [or sister] is born for adversity." What does that mean? Adversity means trouble, testing, or hard times. It's difficult to go through a serious problem by yourself. What a blessing to have a brother or sister with whom you can share your hardship. Having another opinion is very helpful, but having a partner, who will walk through your trial with you, is even more powerful. They can encourage you not to give up.

WHAT DO YOU THINK?

1. When you say critical and hurtful words to your brother or sister, what negative effect can that have on them?

2. A habit is something that if we do it enough times, becomes an automatic reaction. How does developing a habit in the way we speak to our brothers and sisters fit in with today's verse?

3. Can you think of a time when your brother or sister defended you with their words in front of other people, or when you did that for one of your family?

ANSWERS TO YOUR QUESTIONS

1. *When brothers and sisters say hurtful things to each other, it can cause wounds—internal not external—that never heal.*

2. *Today's verse says that brothers and sisters are "born for adversity." In other words, they have a special opportunity to be a source of strength and encouragement to their family. However, if they develop a habit of constantly being critical, they rob their family of this blessing.*

3. *Personal opinion. You may want to ask each child.*

141

60. HOW A "SCROOGE" MET HIS MATCH

He who has a crooked mind finds no good, and he who is perverted [filthy] in his language falls into evil.
Proverbs 17:20

Whenever I hear the term "a crooked mind," I think of a foolish man named Nabal, who lived during the time of the psalmist David. He is a perfect example of how a crooked mind and perverted (filthy) language are usually found together. The Bible describes Nabal and his wife this way: "And the woman (Abigail) was intelligent and beautiful in appearance, but the man was harsh and evil in his dealings" (1 Samuel 25:3). My first question is how in the world did they ever get together?

David and his band of warriors were running from King Saul. Exhausted and hungry, they happened upon Nabal, a wealthy man with plenty of sheep. They respectfully asked him if he could donate some food and drink to the future king of Israel and his men.

Instead of offering to help them, we read, "But Nabal answered David's servants, and said, 'Who is David...Shall I then take my bread and my water and my meat that I have slaughtered for my shearers, and give it to men whose origin I do not know?'" (1 Samuel 25:10, 11). He sounds more like Ebenezer Scrooge or the Grinch.

In response, David and his six hundred warriors decide to go and teach Nabal a serious lesson in good manners.

When Abigail hears that her husband has acted so unwisely and David is on the warpath, she gathers lots of food together and heads for the hungry men. She falls face down before David, apologizes for her husband's behavior, and offers her generous gifts. David is so impressed with her kindness that he spares Nabal's life. God eventually deals with Nabal Himself and takes his life through a heart attack. Later, David marries Abigail because of her wisdom and beauty.

There are plenty of Nabals in our own world who are cruel and selfish. Because their minds are not Christ-centered, their thoughts and actions reflect the condition of their unbelieving hearts. Almost anywhere we go, we hear people cursing God's name and using filthy words.

I think the only thing worse than hearing an unbeliever talk this way is to hear a Christian profane [curse] the name of Jesus or use words that are evil or dirty. Let's ask our Savior to help us always use language that honors His worthy name. Proverbs 4:23 says, "Watch over your heart with all diligence, for from it flow the springs of life."

WHAT DO YOU THINK?

1. Describe Nabal and then describe his wife Abigail.

2. How did Abigail demonstrate that she was a wise woman? How did Nabal demonstrate he had a crooked mind?

3. Perverted or filthy language comes out of some people's mouths. The mouth itself isn't the real source of trouble. What is?

ANSWERS TO YOUR QUESTIONS

1. *Nabal was a proud and greedy man. He had no desire to help others—even those in need. Abigail, on the other hand, was intelligent and beautiful.*

2. *When Abigail heard that Nabal had acted so foolishly toward David, she brought the future king food and asked him not to harm her husband. When David's servants asked Nabal for food to feed the army of 600 men, Nabal mocked them and refused to give them anything.*

3. *In Matthew 12:34, we read that Jesus told the Pharisees, "For the mouth speaks out of that which fills the heart." In other words, our problem is with our heart and mind, not with our mouth.*

61. RUNNING TO MY STRONG TOWER

The name of the Lord is a strong tower; the righteous runs into it and is safe.

Proverbs 18:10

Have you ever been through a hurricane? On August 14, 2004, the eye of Hurricane Charley came right through our town of Debary, Florida.

It formed just off the coast of Africa, crossed the Atlantic, took a sharp right turn around the southern tip of Florida, and blew up the west coast of the Sunshine State. This category 4 hurricane made another right turn at Port Charlotte, Florida, reaching speeds of 150 miles-per-hour at its peak.

Amazingly, Charley seemed to follow Interstate-4 in a north-easterly direction through Orlando, and went right through our town before exiting the state at Daytona Beach. Along the way, it caused 10 deaths and $15.4 billion in damage.[3]

We watched on TV as Charley barreled toward us. Thankfully, the circular winds slowed a little before they hit our town. We could feel and hear the force of the storm as it battered our house. When I first looked outside, the tree in our front yard was bent over to the left. Suddenly, everything was still. When I looked outside again, the same tree that was bent over was now standing erect and the leaves were barely moving. The *eye of the storm* was passing over us. Within minutes, the trailing edge of the hurricane blew by, and our tree bent the opposite way. We lost electricity for a few days, but rejoiced that our house stood strong. It was our refuge and strong tower, and we thanked the Lord for how well built it was.

Today's verse says that the Lord's name is a strong tower or fort to those who are believers in Jesus Christ. How sad that unbelievers have no spiritual tower to run to when they experience storms in their lives. They are forced to face the pain and trials all on their own, without the comfort of the Savior's strong arms.

What do you do when a "Hurricane Charley experience" comes into your life? Do you immediately run to Jesus? It would be a shame to be a child of God and not turn to Him for help.

I love to hold on to Isaiah 41:10 as my strong tower when I'm facing a storm. It says, "Do not fear, for I am with you; do not anxiously look about you, for I am your God. I will strengthen you, surely I will help you, surely I will uphold you with My righteous right hand."

WHAT DO YOU THINK?

1. Can you describe what a hurricane is like? What two directions do the winds move?

2. Can you think of a storm in your life when you prayed to the Lord as your strong tower and He answered by working things out for you?

3. Psalm 66:18 says, "If I regard wickedness in my heart, the Lord will not hear." How does that verse fit in with today's lesson?

ANSWERS TO YOUR QUESTIONS

1. *Hurricane winds usually blow in a circular pattern and also forward.*

2. *Personal opinion. You may want to ask each child.*

3. *God chooses not to hear unbelievers' prayers because they are not His children, unless they are praying to receive Jesus as their Savior.*

62. GOD DELIGHTS IN THE HUMBLE

Before destruction the heart of man is haughty [proud], but humility goes before honor.
Proverbs 18:12

The Bible contains many stories about haughty or proud people who only loved themselves. It also tells stories of humble people who loved God. Let's look at an example of each.

I'm sure God was very careful who He chose to be the earthly parents of His beloved Son Jesus. We learn quite a bit in the Gospels about Mary, who gave birth to Jesus, but very little about His earthly father Joseph. From the few verses that mention him, we gather that he was a humble young man who honored God and wanted to do His will.

Joseph was engaged to be married to Mary, when he learned that she was expecting a baby. He knew he was not the father. But rather than get angry and abandon Mary, Joseph thought of her reputation more than his own. He found a location where Mary would be out of the public eye and not be disgraced or harmed. This tells me he was a loyal and honorable man who was willing to be led by God and not just his own emotions. What's more, his expressions of care happened before he knew that his bride-to-be was carrying the Son of God in her womb.

Within a short period of time, "an angel of the Lord appeared to him in a dream, saying, 'Joseph, son of David, do not be afraid to take Mary as your wife; for that which has been conceived [formed] in her is of the Holy Spirit'" (Matthew 1:20).

In contrast, Herod the Great, who was king during the time of Jesus' birth, was an evil ruler who wanted to destroy God's Son. His grandson, King Herod Agrippa I, was also evil. He thought highly of himself and mistreated Christians in the beginning days of the church.

But something sad happened. "And on an appointed day Herod, having put on his royal apparel, took his seat on the rostrum and began delivering an address to them. And the people kept crying out, 'The voice of a god and not of a man!' And immediately an angel of the Lord struck him [Herod] because he did not give God the glory, and he was eaten by worms and died" (Acts 12:21-23).

You don't have to be a king or queen to be haughty and proud. Many people today ignore God and His love—their personal worlds only revolve around themselves, and there is no room for Jesus in their lives. Even Christians can get their eyes off the Lord and become self-centered. That's pride!

God probably chose Joseph and Mary to be the earthly parents of Jesus because they were humble. What a great honor that would be for anyone. Like today's verse says, "Humility goes before honor."

WHAT DO YOU THINK?

1. After Joseph heard that his fiancée Mary was pregnant, how did he show that he was a humble, God-fearing man?

2. What message did God send to Joseph through an angel, after Joseph acted so kindly to Mary?

3. If the Holy Spirit convicted you as a Christian that you were thinking only of yourself and being proud, what would you need to do to make things right with God?

ANSWERS TO YOUR QUESTIONS

1. *Joseph found a location where Mary would be out of the public eye and would not be disgraced or even harmed.*

2. *God told Joseph through one of His angels that he should not be afraid to marry Mary because the child she was carrying was from the Holy Spirit. It was Jesus Christ Himself.*

3. *Confess your pride to God as sin and accept by faith that He has forgiven you (1 John 1:9).*

63. WHATEVER HAPPPENED TO SOLOMON?

The foolishness of man subverts [ruins] his way, and his heart rages against the Lord.

Proverbs 19:3

In our very first lesson, we read that God told young King Solomon, "Ask what you wish me to give you" (I Kings 3:5). At that point, Solomon loved the Lord and was humble. He chose only "an understanding heart to judge [Your] people [Israel] to discern between good and evil" (verse 9).

God was so pleased with Solomon's unselfish choice that He gave him the wisdom he asked for, and the riches and honor he didn't request. Solomon became the wisest man who ever lived. In fact, later in his reign we learn, "So King Solomon became greater than all the kings of the earth in riches and in wisdom. And all the earth was seeking the presence of Solomon, to hear his wisdom which God had put in his heart" (1 Kings 10:23, 24).

You would expect such an intelligent king to rule Israel with humility and obedience to God throughout his whole reign. Finally, he would go to his grave in honor, leaving a strong nation in the hands of a son, like David had done with him. But unfortunately, that is not what happened.

Instead, toward the end of his life, King Solomon's heart became proud. God told the nation of Israel many times to destroy the pagan nations that occupied the Promised Land. This was to be Israel's land. He told His people not to intermarry with these ungodly people: "For they will turn your sons away from following Me to serve other gods; then the anger of the Lord will be kindled against you, and He will quickly destroy you" (Deuteronomy 7:4).

Solomon apparently thought he knew better than God, because he ignored God's commandment. What we read next is almost impossible to believe. It says, "And he had seven hundred wives, princesses, and three hundred concubines, [or, women who acted like his wives, but were not legally married to the king] and his wives turned his heart away. For it came about when Solomon was old, his wives turned his heart away after other [pagan] gods; and his heart was not wholly devoted to the Lord his God, as the heart of David his father had been (1 Kings 11:3, 4).

God was not pleased with Solomon's disobedience. He told the king that his descendants would no longer rule over Israel. Instead, He would take the kingdom from him and give it to someone else. God followed through on His promise.

How does the story of Solomon apply to us? Well, no matter how smart we are (or think we are), if we become proud and stop obeying God's Word, we are capable of committing the most awful sins imaginable. For God's glory and our good, we would be wise to obey our heavenly Father. Too bad the smartest man who ever lived didn't follow that advice.

WHAT DO YOU THINK?

1. When Solomon first became king, what did he choose when God promised to give him anything he wanted?

2. What was it about Solomon's choice that pleased the Lord? What did God give him in addition to the wisdom he asked for?

3. Why did God want Israel to destroy the nations around them that worshipped idols? How did Solomon's failure to obey God's command by marrying pagan women contribute to Solomon's downfall? What is the lesson for us?

ANSWERS TO YOUR QUESTIONS

1. *Solomon asked God for the ability to rule Israel with wisdom and to judge clearly between right and wrong.*

2. *King Solomon could have asked for riches and power, but he didn't. Instead, he unselfishly asked to be a wise and caring king over God's people. The Lord was so pleased with Solomon's choice that He gave him riches and honor as a bonus on top of the wisdom he asked for.*

3. *God didn't want Israel to worship the idols of the pagan nations. Solomon wanted more and more wives including pagan women, and he ended up following their idols. God knows what is the very best for us, and if we turn our backs on His Word, it could destroy us.*

64. OUR PLANS AND GOD'S GOALS

Many are the plans in a man's heart, but the counsel of the Lord, it will stand.
Proverbs 19:21

When I was a young man in my early twenties, I really thought I was in control of my life and would be able to work wherever I chose. I made my own plans and just expected them to work out. But I forgot one major thing.

As a Christian, my life no longer belonged to me! Jesus bought me with His own blood on Calvary. The Bible says, "Or do you not know that your body is a temple of the Holy Spirit who is in you, whom you have from God, and that you are not your own? For you have been bought with a price: therefore glorify God in your body" (1 Corinthians 6:19, 20).

Just before I graduated from veterinary college in Canada, I accepted a job with a veterinarian in Palatine, Illinois. At the last moment, God turned circumstances around so I ended up moving to East Lansing, Michigan to work at the veterinary clinic at Michigan State University. And I thank the Lord, because that's where I met my wonderful wife. God definitely knows best.

While in Michigan, I applied to a number of human medicine schools, thinking that if I took the training to be an MD, God might use me as a medical missionary. But He closed that door as well.

After working 3½ years at MSU, I received a job offer with a small drug company in Wisconsin. My wife and I prayed about it. God gave us peace in our hearts, so we moved to the town of Grafton, Wisconsin with our two-year-old daughter. We thought we would live there for the rest of our lives.

Proverbs 16:9 says, "The mind of man plans his way, but the Lord directs his steps." I thought the Lord had moved us there so I could work for this company until retirement. But God had another plan in mind. Through a local church, we met some missionary candidates in training with New Tribes Mission. Their down-to-earth love for the Lord impressed us as did their desire to take the gospel to places on earth where it had never gone before.

We soon learned that there were over 2000 different people groups around the world who had never once heard the name of Jesus Christ. The more we learned about these lost tribal groups, the more we realized that this was something worth giving our lives for. We only lived in that town for eighteen months. Prayerfully but fearfully I quit my job, and we were on our way into the missionary training program with NTM.

Looking back, I believe the plans we made *without* the Lord eventually fizzled out. But where the Lord directed us clearly and we followed Him by faith, the doors opened and He guided us. Like today's verse says, many plans are in a man's heart, but the counsel of the Lord will stand.

WHAT DO YOU THINK?

1. Why are Christians not in full charge of their plans for the future?

2. You pray about a decision you have to make and, in time, you have peace about which choice to make and you make it. What would you think if things turn out totally different from your choice? Does it mean that you chose wrongly?

3. What does today's verse mean when it says that the counsel of the Lord will stand?

ANSWERS TO YOUR QUESTIONS

1. *The Bible says that we are not our own, but we are bought with a price—Christ's shed blood on Calvary. (See I Corinthians 6:19, 20)*

2. *No, God heard your prayer, but He had a better plan for you. That's why when Jesus was on earth, even He prayed to his Father, "...yet not as I will, but as [You] [will]" (Matthew 26:39).*

3. *The Lord's choice will be better for us in the long run.*

65. HOW GOOD IS YOUR WORD?

What is desirable in a man is his kindness, and it is better to be a poor man than a liar.
Proverbs 19:22

When you promise to do something for someone, can they be sure you will always follow through on what you said? Maybe you said, "You have my word on it." How much is your word worth?

I've heard people say, "She is as good as her word." This person can be trusted to do what they promise—they will be a loyal friend. The opposite is also true. If you can never count on a person to be at a place at the time they promise, then how can you depend on their word? We would call them unreliable. They may be funny or entertaining, but their word means very little.

Jon, a self-made billionaire, was interviewed on TV recently. Rather than talking about all his money or even about all his shrewd business deals that made him wealthy, he wanted to talk about *keeping your word.*

I remember one story Jon told in particular. He was in the process of selling one of his businesses. He shook hands on the deal and agreed to sell for a certain price. But the lawyers took quite a long time to complete the paperwork. In the meantime, the business increased in value five times. The buyer told Jon that he felt he should pay Jon more money since the business was worth so much more. Jon had every right to accept the extra money, but he told the buyer, "I gave you my word and we shook hands at the lower price, so I'm fine with the amount we agreed on." I could really trust a person like that who values his promises more than money.

But what if someone doesn't keep his word? Is that the same as lying? I've heard people say, "You can't depend on what that person says." It makes me feel that the person can't be trusted. How much better to hear, "Your word is as good as gold." Then friends could always depend on you to do what you promise. That's the kind of friend I want to be. It will also bring glory to our wonderful Savior, Jesus Christ.

WHAT DO YOU THINK?

1. What does it mean when you say, "She is as good as her word"?

2. What are some of the downsides of not keeping your word to other people?

3. Some people believe that you are foolish to keep your promises if it will cost you money. Today's verse says that it's better to be a poor man than a liar. What are your thoughts about each of these two opinions?

ANSWERS TO YOUR QUESTIONS

1. *Her reputation for being trustworthy and reliable depends on how much she keeps her word.*

2. *They are afraid to tell you confidential things. They don't want to hire you for jobs. They are not likely to be a close friend.*

3. *There may be the occasional time when keeping your word will cost you money. In the long run, the rewards will be greater if you have a reputation for keeping your word. Even if it did mean that you were poor as a result of being honest and keeping your word rather than lying, God says, "It is better." I believe He will bless you in other ways, and reward you later in heaven.*

66. WHAT HAVE YOU SEEN OR HEARD LATELY?

The hearing ear and the seeing eye, the Lord has made both of them.
Proverbs 20:12

It amazes me that some people can study about how the five senses work in the human body, and still refuse to believe there is a creator God. They prefer to stubbornly insist that hearing, seeing, tasting, touching, and smelling all appeared by accident.

Hearing and sight are mentioned in today's verse; God made both of them as well as every single cell in our bodies. Can you imagine not being able to hear people talk or listen to music? Or what if you couldn't see the beautiful world around you? Without the sense of taste, food would have no flavor. How boring! We could hurt ourselves badly on something hot or sharp if we had no sense of touch. And finally there is smell. Who doesn't enjoy sniffing a rose or a freshly baked loaf of bread?

Did you know that your ear doesn't actually hear? It's your brain, locked away in the boney shell of your skull, which actually processes the information it receives from those funny shaped ears on each side of your head and hears the sounds. And then it passes on the information to your mind which tells you what to do with it. Delicate little hairs and precision-like structures just inside your outer ear pick up vibrations and sound waves in your environment, convert them to electrical impulses, and transport them along nerve strands to your brain.

The same thing is true of your sight—it's your brain that sees, not your eyeballs. Those two colored balls under your eyebrows simply pick up information in front of you and pass it on to your brain. Every second, thousands of images bombard the retina at the back of the eyeball where they are transformed into electrical charges. These micro-units of energy pass along the delicate nerve fibers to the brain, which then sorts out the millions of images into sensible, 3-D pictures in all their natural colors. When you turn your head, this process begins all over again.

What a marvel the brain is! It not only deals with millions of bits of information from your five senses, but from every other area of your body. Even while you're watching and hearing a brilliant fireworks display, your mind can be thinking about how hard the bench is you are sitting on, or how you wished you had worn a jacket because your skin is cold.

So many parts of our bodies seem to be there for our enjoyment and protection. God designed us with His love for us in mind. Every time we examine an orchid or watch the sun set over a lake, we ought to praise our glorious heavenly Father—the Creator of our universe.

WHAT DO YOU THINK?

1. Do you remember what the five senses are?

2. In what way does your brain actually do the *seeing* rather than your eyeballs?

3. What does it mean to you personally that God made you with not only the five senses, but with every other amazing function of your body?

ANSWERS TO YOUR QUESTIONS

1. *Seeing, hearing, touching, smelling, and tasting.*

2. *The eyeball picks up the images in front of it, where they are converted into electrical impulses and transported to the brain along the two optic nerves. It's the brain that makes sense of all the information it receives.*

3. *Personal opinion. It means that He loves me and wants to have a deep friendship with me. Because God loves mankind, He not only wants to protect us from harm, but He wants us to be able to enjoy the rest of His creation.*

67. WATCH YOUR LANGUAGE!

He who curses his father or his mother, his lamp will go out in time of darkness.

Proverbs 20:20

A few years before David became king of Israel, God chose a priest named Eli to lead the nation spiritually. Apparently Eli did not raise his sons Hophni and Phinehas the way God wanted him to, because the Bible says, "Now the sons of Eli were worthless men; they did not know the Lord" (1 Samuel 2:12). How sad that this man was chosen by God to be a spiritual leader, and yet he failed to teach his own sons to obey the Lord.

When the Jewish people brought animal sacrifices to the tabernacle, it was the priest's job to guide them in following God's specific commandments. Hophni and Phinehas greedily took the best of the animals for themselves—even by force if necessary. And there is no record that Eli ever corrected them: "Thus the sin of the young men was very great before the Lord, for the men despised [hated] the offering of the Lord" (1 Samuel 2:17). The people began to dread going to the tabernacle.

It wasn't until Eli was very old and the local gossip about his immoral sons reached his ears that he finally said to them, "Why do you do such things, the evil things that I hear from all these people? No, my sons; for the report is not good which I hear the Lord's people circulating" (1 Samuel 2:23, 24).

Did Hophni and Phinehas change their evil behavior? The next verse says, "But they would not listen to the voice of their father."

Because God is holy, He could not allow the immorality of Eli's sons to continue unpunished. God told Eli that his refusal to correct his sons showed they were more important to him than He was. When the boys cursed their father, they were also cursing God.

The Lord told Eli that He would correct Hophni and Phinehas Himself by taking their lives on the same day. Sure enough, a couple of chapters later we read, "So the Philistines fought and Israel was defeated, and every man fled to his tent, and the slaughter was very great; for there fell of Israel thirty thousand foot soldiers. And the ark of God was taken; and the two sons of Eli, Hophni and Phinehas, died" (1 Samuel 4:10, 11).

Does God care how children talk and act toward their parents? I think the story of Hophni and Phinehas convinces us that He does care very much. Children bring God joy when they obey their parents with a good heart attitude. In the New Testament it says, "Children, obey your parents in the Lord, for this is right. Honor your father and mother (which is the first commandment with a promise), that it may be well with you, and that you may live long on the earth" (Ephesians 6:1-3).

WHAT DO YOU THINK?

1. Eli was the main priest chosen by God, to guide Israel's worship of Him. In what major area did Eli fail?

2. How do we know that God is pleased when children honor their parents by obeying them?

3. The disobedience of Hophni and Phinehas not only affected them and their father, but many others also. How so?

ANSWERS TO YOUR QUESTIONS

1. *Eli failed to correct his two sons and teach them to follow God.*

2. *God says in His Word that it pleases Him when children obey their parents. For example, in today's story, the Lord punished Eli the priest for not training his children to obey Him. He also punished Hophni and Phinehas for not obeying their dad.*

3. *The behavior of Eli's sons was so awful that it caused the nation of Israel to hate going to the tabernacle with their offerings to worship God.*

68. DON'T BELIEVE YOUR TV!

He who loves pleasure will become a poor man; he who loves wine and oil will not become rich.
Proverbs 21:17

A large percentage of advertising on TV, in magazines, and on the Internet is a big fat lie. The company paying for the ads is not trying to show you the pros and cons of buying their product. They have one goal in mind—to make you feel like you just cannot live a happy life unless you rush out right now and buy it. How many times have you heard an advertiser say, "And if you call this number right now, we will double the offer"?

Nowhere is deceptive advertising more forceful than in beer and liquor commercials. Beer companies sponsor many major sporting events. It's interesting what they *do* show and what they *do not* show.

First, what do these ads do to try and convince you to buy their beer? The commercial often shows an attractive group of young people who appear to be partying and having tremendous fun—maybe dancing in a luxurious house, or playing volleyball on a beach. The advertiser wants young people to identify with this group of "twenty-somethings" and imagine themselves there on the beach too. But we forget that they are only actors being paid to do this one-minute ad.

The commercial does *not* show: a husband who starts drinking alcohol in college, but once married with a family, can't control his drinking. He beats his wife when he's drunk and terrorizes his children. Eventually, he loses his job through his alcoholism, and his wife leaves him to protect her children and herself. Finally one day, in a drunken, guilty stupor, the man who is now homeless takes his own life. Where does this all too common scenario appear in the beer commercial?

Here's another scenario. Dad, mom, and the kids are spending a Friday night together, having devotions, playing board games, eating popcorn, and watching a wholesome movie. They laugh, tease, and enjoy each other. This very satisfying entertainment builds positive memories that last a lifetime. It's interesting that beer companies don't use wholesome scenes like this to advertise their product.

There's nothing ungodly about enjoying other people's company and having fun—even playing beach volleyball. Today's verse, however, makes it very plain that if we live for "questionable fun"—that involves alcohol, drugs, and other chemicals that numb the mind—it almost certainly spells our destruction. Why not live for God's glory? When we do that, He will creatively bless us with "real pleasures."

WHAT DO YOU THINK?

1. What is the typical goal of commercials on TV, in magazines, and on the Internet?

2. How do beer and liquor companies generally picture those who buy their product?

3. What are two scenarios that alcohol-related commercials do *not* show?

ANSWERS TO YOUR QUESTIONS

1. *It's to try and make us believe that we cannot live a happy life unless we buy their product right now (before we forget or talk ourselves out of it.)*

2. *They choose actors for the commercials who appear to be young, attractive, wealthy, and with very few moral boundaries or limits to their actions.*

3. *They do not show a picture of alcoholism that is very common in our world. It may begin in college, but ends in wife and child abuse, loss of one's job, divorce, homelessness, drug use, and even death. They also don't show a stable, happy family spending quality time together and building wonderful memories that last a lifetime—without chemicals that numb their minds.*

69. THINK BEFORE YOU SPEAK!

He who guards his mouth and his tongue, guards his soul from troubles.
                                                    Proverbs 21:23

When I was a boy, I read a fairy tale about a king and his court jester or clown. The jester was supposed to tell jokes and funny stories, but only when the king was sad. But the jester had a problem. He couldn't turn off the jokes and puns. [A *pun* is a joke that depends on a specific word that has several meanings.] Finally, the king got so tired of his foolishness that he told his punster, "If you tell one more pun, I'm going to hang you."

For several weeks the jester restrained himself from telling any jokes and puns. The king even began to wonder if he had been too harsh, so he told his jester that he would not hang him. The jester replied without thinking, "No noose is good news!" The king changed his mind again.

I believe the lesson in today's verse is that we all should think for a brief moment before we speak. At times I've wished I could take back my quick comments, but I had already done the damage.

Think about the following types of people and the unwise statements they make. Ask yourself honestly if you usually guard your mouth, or if you talk like any of them:

1. CRITICAL CARL – Do you know someone who constantly criticizes other people? It's like Carl's mind has only one track. Even when those around him do things that deserve praise, Carl manages to think of something negative and says it.

2. GOSSIPY GWEN – All of us are tempted to pass along juicy tidbits of information about people, even when we've been asked to keep them confidential. Gwen gives in to the temptation because she likes others to think that she knows a lot—even when it means hurting her friends.

3. LYING LINDA – In order to be the center of attention, Linda likes to add untrue details to a story. It's become such a habit that she lies even when she doesn't need to. Now she's losing

friends because they just can't tell when Linda is telling the truth or not.

4. DIRTY-TALK DARYL – Somehow Daryl has gotten hold of some wrong information. He thinks that for a fellow to be tough and manly he has to talk dirty and curse a lot. You know what? This only shows that Daryl has been misinformed and he lacks self-control.

God is giving us wise advice when He tells us to guard our mouths. When we stop and think before we speak, it not only pleases our heavenly Father, but we'll also discover that it pleases our friends also.

WHAT DO YOU THINK?

1. What should we do before we speak?

2. How do people often react to someone like "Critical Carl" who always seems to find the negative side of others and states it?

3. Our mouths and tongues are not the actual problem, are they? What is?

ANSWERS TO YOUR QUESTIONS

1. *We should think about what we're going to say, to be sure our words are not going to hurt people.*

2. *They get turned off and get tired of being around Carl. They don't want to be a close friend.*

3. *Our minds are what decide the things we say. Our mouths simply state what our minds are thinking.*

70. ARGUING WITH GOD

There is no wisdom and no understanding and no counsel against the Lord.
Proverbs 21:30

Do you ever wish you could sit across the dinner table from God and talk to Him frankly? Maybe you would like to ask Him why He allowed you to get so painfully sick when you didn't do anything wrong to deserve it. Or why your special pet died. Or why at times it seems the more you try to be a good person, the more things go wrong. Surely if God would just listen to your good reasons, He would be convinced and make things better for you in the future.

Job, a godly man in the Old Testament, was given that opportunity. You will want to read the book of Job to get the whole story, but he was one of the most faithful men of his time—and wealthy.

The Bible says that Satan approached God one day to complain that Job was a righteous man only because God was always protecting him from harm. If bad things happened, he said, then Job would act differently. For God's own reasons, He allowed Satan to torment Job with one nightmarish calamity after another. Enemies stole all his oxen and donkeys, then killed his servants. Fire from heaven destroyed Job's entire flock of sheep and every shepherd but one. Other enemies took his 3,000 camels and killed almost all the workers. When all Job's children were together at a party, a great wind caused the roof to collapse on them and they were all killed. And all this bad news came to Job within a few hours.

How do you think Job reacted to this avalanche of misery? Did he explode in anger and throw a tantrum against God for being so mean to him? No, he worshiped God! In fact he blessed God's name. The Bible says, "Through all this Job did not sin nor did he blame God" (Job 1:22).

Just when you think that things couldn't get any worse, Job's wife came along and said, "Do you still hold fast your integrity? Curse God and die!" Wow! What a positive encouragement she was! Job replied, "'Shall we indeed accept good from God and not accept adversity?' In all this Job did not sin with his lips" (Job 2:10b).

Was that the end of Job's misery? Not at all! For the next thirty-five chapters, his friends sit with him in his miserable condition and try to convince him that this nightmare he was experiencing had to be because of some hidden area of sin. There wasn't a happy encourager in the group.

At the end of this exciting book, God speaks to Job. Instead of answering all Job's questions, He reminds him that He is the Creator of the universe, owns all things, and by His mighty power causes them to work. In the end, God rewards Job because he remained faithful to Him. He received double the wealth he had before and even lived another 140 years.

Today's verse says that no one can stand before God as an equal in wisdom, understanding, or counsel. Job thought he could change God's mind through arguing his opinion, but he soon learned differently.

WHAT DO YOU THINK?

1. If Jesus was physically in the room with you now, and you could ask Him only one question, what would it be?

2. God allowed Satan to test Job in certain areas, but not in others. What does this teach us about Satan's influence in our lives?

3. Instead of God answering Job's questions, the Lord described how powerful He was, particularly in creating and controlling the universe. Can you think of a reason why God's response was wiser than simply answering Job's questions?

ANSWERS TO YOUR QUESTIONS

1. *Ask each child for their personal choices.*

2. *It shows that Satan can only affect God's children to the extent that God allows him. He does not have any more power than is permitted by God.*

3. *By God revealing to Job how great, majestic, and powerful He is, He was showing that He is the answer to every question that Job or anyone else will ever have. Job needed to keep trusting God and His holy nature. Job did trust God, and the Lord blessed him abundantly for his faith.*

71. BE CAREFUL WHERE YOU HANG OUT!

He who sows iniquity will reap vanity [emptiness], and the rod of his fury will perish.

Proverbs 22:8

God mentions a number of creepy characters in the Bible. One of the worst was a man named Haman. We find him in the book of Esther, slithering his way up the corporate ladder of the Gentile King Ahasuerus. This wealthy and powerful king ruled the Middle East from India to Ethiopia, hundreds of years before Jesus was born.

The story begins with the king firing queen Vashti, because she insulted him publicly. He devises a plan similar to the Miss America contest to find the most beautiful young lady in his whole kingdom to be his new queen.

At this point, we are introduced to Esther, the very attractive niece of Mordecai, both of whom are Jews. (God never stopped loving the nation of Israel, even though they constantly turned their backs on Him.) The Lord guides Esther to find favor with the king's officials. She is also given special advantages in this royal beauty contest.

Can you believe that all of the young ladies in this competition had a whole year of preparation before they first met the king? They had, "six months with oil of myrrh and six months with spices and the cosmetics for women" (Esther 2:12b). That's a lot of Avon products!

The king eventually chooses Esther to be his new queen. It's about this time that we first meet Haman. This slippery little man becomes so powerful in the king's court that the king orders the local people to bow down and honor him whenever he is present. Mordecai, Esther's uncle, refuses to bow down to Haman, and word soon spreads.

Haman is furious. So he begins plotting to kill Mordecai as well as every other Jew in the kingdom. Haman even convinces the king to order every official throughout the kingdom, to destroy all Jews—men, women, and children—and seize their possessions. Apart from God, things look bleak for the nation of Israel.

Mordecai realizes that Esther may be Israel's only hope, so he sends a servant to tell her, "And who knows whether you have not attained royalty for such a time as this" (Esther 4:14b)? Esther knows that no one, including the queen, can approach the king unless they are invited. To do so means certain death. But Esther loves her Jewish people more than her own life, so she sends word back to her uncle, "And thus I will go in to the king, which is not according to the law; and if I perish, I perish" (Esther 4:16b). What a courageous young woman!

Esther invites her husband the king and wicked Haman to a banquet where she exposes Haman's evil plan to kill off the Jewish people. What does the king do? He orders Haman to be hanged on the very gallows he had built for Mordecai.

Be sure to read the whole exciting story! And while you're at it, notice the truth of today's verse that says, "He who sows iniquity will reap vanity [emptiness]."

WHAT DO YOU THINK?

1. What kind of sin in Haman's life most contributed to his downfall?

2. How did Esther respond to Mordecai when he told her that she may have attained royalty "for such a time as this"? She would have to risk death by going to the king uninvited, to save the nation of Israel from being murdered.

3. 1 Peter 5:6 says, "Humble yourselves, therefore, under the mighty hand of God, that He may exalt you at the proper time." How are Esther and Mordecai's lives an example of this verse?

ANSWERS TO YOUR QUESTIONS

1. *Pride. When the king placed Haman in a high position of authority, it apparently went to his head. He then wanted everyone to bow before him as if he was the king himself. When Mordecai refused to bow down, evil Haman not only plotted to kill Mordecai, but the whole Jewish nation. God then used Esther to foil his murderous plan. Haman's pride caused his own destruction.*

2. *Esther said she would go in to ask the king to spare the Jewish people and, "If I perish, I perish."*

3. *Esther put the safety of the Jewish nation before her own, and God used her to rescue His people. The Lord took this young Jewish girl who very few people knew, and placed her as queen of a vast area. Mordecai was a humble Jewish man who refused to bow his knees to wicked Haman. He would only give such honor to the God of Israel. Because of his courage and concern for his people, God placed him in a high place of honor in the king's court.*

72. MORE THAN A FOOTBALL

He who loves purity of heart and whose speech is gracious, the king is his friend.

Proverbs 22:11

God is eager to find courageous people who will show His power in how they live. To some of His devoted children He gives fame, wealth, and power as a platform to testify of His greatness. Others faithfully show His greatness by their humble lifestyle. In both cases, the Lord Jesus is honored.

I have followed one young man through his college career who has been blessed by God in a number of ways. Tim Tebow is considered by some to be the greatest football player to ever play at the college level. What is even more amazing is his Christian testimony and how he constantly shared his love for Christ.

First, let's look at Tim's football career at University of Florida:

1. His 4-year statistics were nothing short of amazing. In his 55 games as quarterback, Tim threw for 9,286 yards, scoring 88 TD's with only 15 interceptions. He ran the ball himself for 2,947 yards with 57 touchdowns.

2. Here are just a few of the awards he won:
    - First team All American (2007, 2008)
    - First team All SEC (2007, 2008, 2009)
    - Associated Press Player of the Year (2007)
    - Heisman Trophy (2007)
    - ESPY Award for Best Male College Athlete (2008, 2009).[4]

Even more outstanding is Tim's Christian testimony:

1. Whenever I've heard him interviewed on TV after a football game, his first words were, "I want to thank my Lord and Savior Jesus Christ."

2. During the three summers before entering college, Tim worked with his missionary parents in the orphanage they ran in the Philippines.

3. He was the first home-schooled athlete and first college sophomore to win the Heisman Trophy.
4. During one of the three Heisman Trophy presentations he attended, a short documentary clip showed him sharing the gospel with a large group of prisoners. He even had an "altar call" at the end for those who wanted to receive Christ, and some responded.
5. During his games, he usually wore a Bible verse reference in white on his black eye paint.

What does all of this mean? God will not necessarily give to every Christian athlete such prominence and success that He has to Tebow. But as I watched Tim give the closing prayer at the National Prayer Breakfast in Washington D.C. on February 4, 2010—where he sat at the head table with President Obama and other famous people—I couldn't help but think of today's verse. For sure Tim has used his popularity and his athletic skills as a platform to profess his faith in Jesus Christ. The Lord, in turn, has honored his testimony and allowed him to be a "friend of kings."

WHAT DO YOU THINK?

1. What usually were Tim Tebow's first words when he was interviewed by the press after one of his football games?

2. What does it mean to love purity of heart? What does being gracious of speech mean?

3. Since God doesn't make every one of His children as famous as Tim Tebow, how are we supposed to have an impact on our world if we just lead "ordinary" lives?

ANSWERS TO YOUR QUESTIONS

1. *Tim would say, "I want to thank my Lord and Savior Jesus Christ."*

2. *To love "purity of heart" means to delight in pleasing God by obeying His Word and professing the greatness of Jesus Christ at every opportunity. When such a person sins, they confess their sin to God right away. "Gracious of speech" means to talk kindly, humbly, and without prideful boasting.*

3. *Actually, God doesn't have any "ordinary kids." We are all made by Him to be unique and different. The Lord just wants us to be faithful and obedient to Him where we are. Then He can use us as He desires. Some of the people who have had the greatest impact on my life were only known by a small circle of people.*

73. WHAT DO YOU MEAN I CAN'T EAT?

Do not associate with a man given to anger; or go with a hot-tempered man, lest you learn his ways, and find a snare for yourself.
Proverbs 22:24, 25

Angry people make foolish choices. Instead of patiently thinking and praying about a decision, they react according to their emotions—often in childish and unreasonable ways.

Saul, Israel's first king, was an angry man. Time and again he refused to obey God and insisted on his own stubborn way. He was also jealous of David who seemed to be everything Saul wished to be.

There is one incident that happened early in Saul's reign—even before David killed Goliath—that demonstrates Saul's angry personality. Israel has been at war with the Philistines for some time. Jonathan, Saul's son, trusts God and wins an amazing victory against an enemy garrison, with only his armor-bearer to help him. Too bad his father Saul didn't have that kind of courage.

For no good reason other than his own pride, Saul makes up a foolish rule, probably during a fit of anger. The Bible explains, "Now the men of Israel were hard-pressed on that day, for Saul had put the people under oath, saying, 'Cursed be the man who eats food before evening, and until I have avenged myself on my enemies.' So none of the people tasted food" (1 Samuel 14:24). The soldiers need food to keep up their strength, but the king can only think of himself and getting revenge. While Saul's army is crashing through the forest in search of the enemy, they spot a bee nest dripping with honey. Jonathan, who did not hear his father's order, dips the end of his spear in the honey and eats the sweet syrup like a Popsicle.

The good news is that he brightens up right away with renewed energy. The bad news is that someone had to inform him: "Your father strictly put the people under oath, saying, 'Cursed be the man who eats food today.' And the people were weary" (1 Samuel 14:28). So Jonathan's life is threatened and the

172

soldiers grow more weary and hungry. When they are next able to overpower the enemy, the Bible says that they rushed greedily upon their livestock, killed them, and ate them without first draining their blood, as God's law required.

Anger can lead people to make sinful choices. Let's review:

1. Saul orders his soldiers not to eat anything before evening and until he avenges himself on his enemies or the soldiers will be cursed and killed.

2. The king fails to inform his son Jonathan of the order, so the young warrior eats some honey he finds in the forest.

3. The soldiers become so weary from lack of food that when they win the next battle, they immediately kill and eat some of the enemy's livestock without draining their blood as God's law requires.

4. The men in Saul's army lose total respect for their king and refuse to obey his foolish order. They rescue Jonathan so he can stay alive.

Can you see why God tells us in today's verses not to associate with angry people?

WHAT DO YOU THINK?

1. As you think about King Saul's order—"Cursed be the man who eats food before evening, and until I have avenged myself on my enemies"—what clue shows that this order was from Saul and not God?

2. Why do you think the army of Israel stood up for Jonathan and wouldn't let his father kill him?

3. What is one lesson *all* dads can learn from this story?

ANSWERS TO YOUR QUESTIONS

1. *Saul's reason for the order was self-centered. He wanted his own revenge rather than God's glory.*

2. *The soldiers knew Saul and Jonathan very well. They had seen Jonathan trust God to attack an enemy fortress with only one other person, because he trusted the Lord to help him. Saul, on the other hand, was an angry man who made foolish and childish decisions, even though he was king. The army was not about to let Jonathan die because of such an unwise order.*

3. *There are many lessons fathers can learn here. One in particular is that fathers are not only to love and train their children, but to be a godly example to them. Children often learn more by observing actions than by hearing someone talk. As fathers (and mothers) live under the control of the Holy Spirit, Jesus Christ will express His loving life through them. He will also help them make wise decisions.*

74. DON'T LET MONEY BECOME YOUR BOSS!

Do not weary yourself to gain wealth, cease from your consideration of it. When you set your eyes on it, it is gone. For wealth certainly makes itself wings, like an eagle that flies toward the heavens.

Proverbs 23:4, 5

The year 2009 was a very difficult one financially for the whole world. Some called it a "global recession." World leaders met several times to discuss ways to prevent the total collapse of their economies. No country escaped rising debt or loss of jobs. In the USA and Canada, many people lost one third or more of their retirement savings in a few months. Like today's verses explain, their wealth made itself "wings, like an eagle that flies toward the heavens."

The Bible has a lot to say about money—because it's important to us. Can you think of two people during Jesus' days on earth, who had an unhealthy desire for money? We can learn a lot from Zaccheus and Judas Iscariot.

Luke tells us that Zaccheus was a little Jewish man and a chief tax gatherer for the Romans who were in control of Israel. He was rich, probably because he collected some money on the side for himself. Zaccheus was eager to see Jesus, the worker of miracles, when He passed through his home town. Because he was short, he climbed a sycamore tree to get a better view.

Jesus not only knew who Zaccheus was, but He knew this man worshipped his wealth. The Lord looked up into the tree and said, "Zaccheus, hurry and come down, for today I must stay at your house" (Luke 19:5). He wasted no time in climbing down, and he received Jesus gladly. Zaccheus must have opened his heart to the Savior fully realizing that He was the long expected Messiah. The little man's heart melted and he promised to give half of his possessions to the poor. If he cheated any others, he would repay them four times what he took from them.

Judas Iscariot was a different type—he wanted to become rich regardless of how crooked he had to be. As one of Jesus' twelve disciples, he had the privilege to hear and watch the Lord

175

day after day for three years. Yet he was obsessed with how to get his greedy hands on money. Jesus knew exactly what Judas was up to. But he gave Judas many opportunities to change his mind and confess his sin of greed.

What a loving Savior He is! Even when Jesus announced to all twelve of the disciples at the last Passover supper before His death, "Truly I say to you that one of you will betray Me" (Matthew 26:21b), all Judas could think of was the thirty pieces of silver he would gain from betraying Jesus. Later, he identified Jesus to the chief priests and elders by approaching and kissing Him—a common greeting of that day. He sold out his best friend. But he died in shame and guilt. Zaccheus, however, saw the error of his ways and made Jesus the center of his life.

So, is money evil? Of course not—we need it to live. It's only when we put our earthly treasures before the Lord Jesus and His will for us that we get into trouble. Money comes and goes, but the Christian life is forever.

WHAT DO YOU THINK?

1. Is money evil? When does earning money become wrong?

2. Explain the difference in how Zaccheus thought about money once he met Jesus, and how Judas thought.

3. If you had the opportunity to talk to Judas right now, knowing what you do about him, what would you say that might be a help to him?

ANSWERS TO YOUR QUESTIONS

1. *Gathering earthly treasure of any kind only becomes wrong when we put that before the Lord Jesus and His will for us. The money itself doesn't sin; our hearts do. Many people spend their whole lives trying to gather as much money as they can, and will do almost anything to get more.*

2. *When Zaccheus met Jesus, he had to know Him better. Knowing that, Jesus told him that He wanted to stay at his house. Luke 19:6 says that Zaccheus received Jesus gladly. Shortly after that, Zaccheus was convicted in his heart of having cheated people on their taxes, so he promised to pay them back four times. Also, he determined to give one half of his wealth to the poor. Judas, on the other hand, travelled with Jesus for three years and saw the Savior doing miracles constantly. He had to know that Jesus was the expected Messiah. But greed for money corrupted his heart, so that all he could think of was how he could get thirty pieces of silver by betraying Christ to the high priest.*

3. *Personal opinion. You may want to ask each child.*

75. ALWAYS CHOOSE THE TRUTHFUL WAY!

Buy truth, and do not sell it, get wisdom and instruction and understanding.

Proverbs 23:23

What in the world does it mean to "buy truth, and do not sell it"? It means to make every effort to tell and live the truth—and never sell out your honest reputation for anything. Every word we speak and every choice we make should be truthful. In addition, we should seek after wisdom, instruction, and clear understanding.

Real life is often more interesting than fiction. One of my favorite stories in the Old Testament is nothing less than outstanding. The region of Samaria, where the king of Israel and other Jews are living, is experiencing a great famine. The pagan king of Aram decides to attack them, so his army surrounds the walled city, aiming to starve the residents into submission. The people eat some horrible things as they try to survive.

We then meet four male lepers sitting at the entrance gate to the city. They say to one another, "Why do we sit here until we die?" (2 Kings 7:3). They have only two choices: Go further into the city and starve with the rest of the citizens, or walk toward the enemy camp and hope they might be spared. They decide, "'Now therefore come, and let us go over to the camp of the Arameans. If they spare us, we shall live; and if they kill us, we shall but die.' And they arose *at twilight* to go to the camp of the Arameans" (2 Kings 7:4b, 5a).

What do you think the lepers find at the enemy camp? No one! God had created a deafening noise that sounded just like chariots, horses, and a huge army. The Arameans imagined that the king of Israel had hired several foreign armies to descend on them and wipe them out. So they fled *in the twilight*, the very time that the four lepers headed for the Arameans' camp.

Imagine the four sickly men hobbling into the enemy camp. They stop in their tracks, eyes and mouths wide open. No one is there! The soldiers had left all their animals, their food, their weapons—everything—and headed for the hills. After the lepers eat their fill, they gather up all the treasure they can carry and hide it. But then a strange thing happens. The men realize they are not "buying the truth"—they are thinking only of themselves by greedily hiding all the treasure and food. The lepers say to each other, "We are not doing right. This day is a day of good news, but we are keeping silent...Now therefore come, let us go and tell the king's household" (2 Kings 7:9). And that's exactly what they did!

So, what is the lesson here? Our dear heavenly Father not only wanted to protect the people of Samaria, but He wanted to teach them about buying the truth and not selling it. The four lepers realized that being greedy and thinking only of themselves was wrong. So, they shared the good news with the rest of the city and became heroes of the day.

WHAT DO YOU THINK?

1. What miracle did God do to defeat the Samaritans' enemy and provide food for them when they were starving?

2. When the lepers realized they were being selfish, they said, "This day is a day of good news, but we are keeping silent...Now therefore come, let us go and tell the king's household." How could this statement also apply to us who are believers in Jesus?

3. What is another way of saying, "Buy the truth and do not sell it"?

ANSWERS TO YOUR QUESTIONS

1. *At the same time that the four lepers approached the enemy camp—twilight—God made an enormous noise like the sound of several armies. The enemy was so frightened that they dropped everything and ran for their lives.*

2. *We have the good news of salvation through Jesus Christ. Today, we should look for opportunities to share the good news with the unsaved, rather than keeping it to ourselves.*

3. *Every word we speak and every choice we make should be truthful. We should be known for being honest—we shouldn't consider being dishonest even for money.*

76. EVERY TEEN NEEDS A COACH/CHEERLEADER

The father of the righteous will greatly rejoice, and he who begets [is the father of] a wise son will be glad in him. Let your father and your mother be glad, and let her rejoice who gave birth to you.
Proverbs 23:24, 25

Parents wear a lot of hats—that means they have a lot of different responsibilities in raising their family. Also, as their children mature, dad and mom lose some of those tasks, but gain new ones. One role that never seems to change for parents is that of being a coach/cheerleader.

A *coach* is an instructor or trainer who caringly teaches another person how to be successful. A *cheerleader* enthusiastically roots for another—encouraging them to keep pressing ahead, to give their very best, and not to quit.

Here are a few areas that teens may want to ask their family "coach/cheerleader" about:

1. how to have personal devotions—to nourish yourself spiritually from the Bible and enjoy fellowship with God
2. the importance of positive friendships—how wrong relationships can ultimately destroy your good name and reputation
3. how to manage your money—saving, budgeting, giving to the Lord's work, simple investing, frugal buying, and banking
4. respecting and honoring your parents. Your words, attitudes, and actions should reflect the treasure they are.
5. the value of a good name—how it takes years to build a reputation of honesty and integrity, and just moments to destroy it
6. how hard work builds character—learning to put yourself wholeheartedly into jobs that may seem unpleasant, without grumbling or quitting
7. the importance of being generous. Sometimes a "tightwad" fools himself into thinking he is just frugal or careful.
8. the dangers of predators of all kinds—scam artists, sexual predators, and internet dangers.

Dad and mom, here are a couple of suggestions in the area of being an effective coach/cheerleader:

1. Listen to your teens. Learn what activities and rites-of-passage are important to them and why. Generational differences are real. Don't always resort to lectures. Learn how to draw out your teens—give them time to reason decisions out personally.

2. Be a real cheerleader! Cultivate good memories. Keep reminding them that you are their biggest fan. Praise and encouragement are "magical."

The apostle Paul wrote some wise words to the Christian family: "*Children*, be obedient to your parents in all things, for this is well-pleasing to the Lord. *Fathers*, do not exasperate [make angry] your children, that they may not lose heart" (Colossians 3:20, 21).

WHAT DO YOU THINK?

1. Why wouldn't parents know everything there is to know about being a teenager, since mom and dad both went through their own teen years?

2. Would you like your parents to help you choose your friends? What would be the main advantages of getting your parents' input on who your closest friends should be? (You may want to let each of your children give their opinion.)

3. God gave us sound family advice through the apostle Paul's letter to the Colossian Christians. What did He say *children* should do and why? What advice did he give to *fathers* and why?

ANSWERS TO YOUR QUESTIONS

1. *First of all, each person was created unique by God, and so would not think exactly like any other person. Also, the world our children face daily bears little resemblance to the world we experienced even one generation ago. Most parents have trouble keeping up with the technology their children think of as routine.*

2. *Personal opinion. You may want to ask each child. Your parents have had a lot of friends over their years of growing up and as adults—some very close friends and others just casual. They have also watched other people's friendships and been able to evaluate those that were positive and others that dragged both parties down. Like a lot of people, you probably want the independence of choosing your own friends, but you would be very wise to at least ask your parents for their input on your friends.*

3. *According to Colossians 3:20, 21, children should obey their parents in all things, because it pleases God. Also, fathers (and mothers too) should not purposely exasperate (or make angry) their children, because it causes the children to feel defeated and "lose heart."*

77. HOW TO HAVE A HAPPY HOME

By wisdom a house is built, and by understanding it is established; and by knowledge the rooms are filled with all precious and pleasant riches.
Proverbs 24:3, 4

One of my earliest memories of a family sitcom on TV was "Ozzie and Harriet"—the Nelson family.[5] The parents and their two sons, David and Ricky, really were a true family, not a made-up one as in today's sitcoms. Whether they acted the same way on TV as they did in real life is hard to know, but they sure seemed to enjoy each other's company.

In some ways the Nelsons did not picture life as it really is. Any problems they faced were minor and could be resolved in a humorous way in thirty minutes—including commercials. We all know that our lives rarely work out that way. Yes, we have great memory-building times, but sooner or later we all experience teeth-rattling trials that take much longer than a half hour to get over.

Is there any formula for a happy home? Only God in His perfect wisdom knows what will contribute most to a successful family where joy and love rule. So let's consider what He has to say to dads, moms, and the kids.

Husbands – "Husbands, *love* your wives, just as Christ also loved the church and *gave* Himself up for her" (Ephesians 5:25). The husband and father sets the tone or attitude in the home. God urges your dad not only to love your mom as much as himself, but to "give" himself. This means he needs to be the spiritual shepherd of your family and put the family's needs before his own.

Wives – "Wives, *be subject* to your own husbands, as to the Lord...and let the wife see to it that she *respect* her husband" (Ephesians 5:22, 33). Even though a wife is equal to her husband in most areas of family authority, God still asks your mom to honor your dad as the family's spiritual head and to give him the respect he needs.

184

Children – "Children, *obey* your parents in the Lord, for this is right. *Honor* your father and mother (which is the first commandment with a promise)" (Ephesians 6:1, 2).

One way of attempting to have a happy home would be to try to imitate a seemingly perfect family on your favorite sitcom. But there's no such thing as a perfect family. Why don't we just follow God's formula that emphasizes wisdom, understanding, and knowledge? After all, He made families, and He really wants dads, moms, and kids to enjoy each other.

WHAT DO YOU THINK?

1. Why isn't the average family sitcom on TV a good example of what most homes are really like?

2. Would trying to imitate a happy family on a TV sitcom be a good idea for a Christian family? Why or why not?

3. What are the children's primary responsibilities in the home, according to what the apostle Paul wrote to the church at Ephesus?

ANSWERS TO YOUR QUESTIONS

1. *Most family TV sitcoms deal with problems and trials that can be resolved in less than thirty minutes. The goal of the TV program is to entertain the public, while the goal of the real family is to honor God and be a testimony to the world.*

2. *There is no such thing as a perfect family. Even the most stable family on TV is a group of actors following a script. God has described simply and clearly what a Christian family should be like. Also, He is there to help you all be what will please and glorify Him. You'll be amazed at how much you will enjoy each other also.*

3. *God says that children are responsible to "obey" their parents in the Lord (or as if they were obeying the Lord.) They could obey with a sour attitude, and this is why God's Word says also that children should "honor" their parents. This means to choose to respect them as God's representatives in your home with a sweet attitude.*

78. HONEY, YOU'RE SO SWEET

My son, eat honey, for it is good, yes, the honey from the comb is sweet to your taste; know that wisdom is thus for your soul; if you find it, then there will be a future, and your hope will not be cut off.
Proverbs 24:13, 14

Do you like to drip honey over toast or fresh biscuits and savor its sweet taste? Honey is good for your health and fun to eat too. Even Winnie-the-Pooh keeps a jar of it on hand.

But do you realize what a complex process our heavenly Father created, so that we can enjoy the delicious flavor? Honeybees work hard gathering nectar from various plants and trees. We can do the same thing by plucking off a lilac blossom and sucking the nectar up like a straw.

God created the honeybee with two stomachs—a regular stomach and a honey stomach to hold the nectar. At times the bee will travel to a thousand flowers or more to fill up its honey stomach. When these honey bees return to the hive, other bees called worker bees suck the nectar out of their special "honey tanks." Then they refine the sweet juice by chewing it. When it's ready for storage—in about one half-hour—these worker bees store the nectar all over the hive in little cells they also make.

But they're not done yet. These little workmen fan the stored nectar with their wings. This causes the water to evaporate from it, and leaves the honey thick and syrupy. The bees put a plug of wax over each cell to hold the honey in. This preserves it until they are ready to eat it—or the beekeeper takes it away.[6]

How does the little honeybee, no longer than one half-inch, know to follow each step in transforming the sweet nectar into delicious honey? Is it just luck, or has our creative heavenly Father programmed this little insect to follow each precise step? Now, what does honey have to do with wisdom?

In today's verses, God points out that as honey is good for our taste and our health, so is wisdom for developing healthy attitudes in our minds and spirits. If we will constantly depend on the Lord for His wishes to be accomplished in our lives, He will reward us with His wisdom. There is a verse we read earlier that explains this principle clearly: "But if any of you lacks wisdom, let him ask of God, who gives to all men [and women and children] generously and without reproach [or scolding], and it will be given to him" (James 1:5).

WHAT DO YOU THINK?

1. Would you explain briefly the process of how bees make honey from flower nectar?

2. To what does today's verse compare the sweet taste of honey?

3. Proverbs 25:16 says, "Have you found honey? Eat only what you need." What does it mean and does it contradict today's verse?

ANSWERS TO YOUR QUESTIONS

1. *The bee gathers nectar from flowers, filling up its honey stomach.*
   - *Other bees in the hive suck the nectar out of the first bee's honey stomach and chew or digest it.*
   - *These worker bees place the nectar around the hive in little cells and then fan it with their wings to thicken it into honey.*
   - *The bees cover each cell containing honey with a wax plug to preserve it until needed.*

2. *Just as honey is sweet to the taste, so is wisdom, which comes from God, to the soul. The quality of our lives depends on the wisdom we gain.*

3. *The new verse means that although honey tastes delicious and it's good for you, you should use self-control and not overeat--even honey. Today's verse compares tasting honey to gaining wisdom from God. The new verse seems to only be cautioning about eating too much honey to the point where it makes you sick. The verses don't contradict each other.*

79. YOU'RE OK, AND I'M OK TOO

He who says to the wicked, "You are righteous," peoples will curse him, nations will abhor him; but to those who rebuke the wicked will be delight, and a good blessing will come upon them.
Proverbs 24:24, 25

Just recently, I watched politicians, athletes, and movie stars stand before the press—really the entire world—and admit they had lied, cheated, stolen, or done something equally sinful. Often the spouse of the guilty person stood beside him as he confessed, looking embarrassed and disappointed. The unfortunate thing is that rarely do they come forward to confess publicly while they are still involved in their sin. They only come clean after some reporter exposes them.

When questioned about their behavior, their first reaction is to strongly deny it. But this makes reporters even more eager to search out the truth. Only when witness after witness confirm that the "star" really is guilty, do we usually see the individual publicly admit it. Next up, we hear other celebrities saying, "We all make mistakes! We're only human! Nobody's perfect!" That's an illustration of the first of today's verses. The second verse promises blessing to the individual who rebukes the wicked person.

King David found himself on the receiving end of just such a rebuke. Instead of being at the head of his army at a time of war, he was lounging around Jerusalem with too much free time on his hands. Because David wasn't looking to God for His will at the time, he followed his own sinful desires and fell deeply into sin. The Bible describes the scene this way: "Then it happened in the spring, at the time when kings go out to battle, that David sent Joab and his servants with him and all Israel, and they destroyed the sons of Ammon and besieged Rabbah. But David stayed at Jerusalem" (2 Samuel 11:1).

Although God called David, "a man after My heart, who will do all My will" (Acts 13:22), David did not always choose to obey God. While in Jerusalem, he chose to covet another man's wife. One sin led to another, and he eventually killed the woman's husband, Uriah, to try and cover it all up.

But God sent a trusted servant, Nathan, to confront David about his sin. God cared for David's well-being and for justice to be done. At one point in the meeting, God's messenger bluntly told the king, "You are the man" (2 Samuel 12:7)!

David was stunned. He knew he was guilty. Then he admitted his sin before God and Nathan. David accepted God's forgiveness, and he decided to obey the Lord from then on.

We may make excuses for our own sin and that of others by saying, "Nobody's perfect!" or, "It's really not your fault." Even unbelievers know such statements are a cover up. God's way is to kindly but truthfully tell a brother or sister in the Lord their sin—privately and honestly. Maybe they will realize their sin and confess it to God. That's what a true friend would do.

WHAT DO YOU THINK?

1. What kinds of excuses do people often make for their friends when their sin comes to light?

2. What is wrong with the thinking behind the above excuses?

3. What kind of attitude should we have when we go to talk to believers who refuse to admit they are walking in sin?

1. *They often make statements like: "Everyone makes mistakes" or, "Nobody is perfect" or, "It's not her fault because..." or, "She's only human."*

2. *These excuses are wrong because they make it sound like the guilty person had no choice but to sin. We know from God's Word that that isn't true. The Lord put the Holy Spirit in each Christian to give them strength against temptation. Even though it's true that the guilty person is "only human," what she has done is still sin against God.*

3. *We should go humbly as a friend and fellow member of the body of Christ. We need to speak graciously but truthfully exactly what we see. Then, we can leave the results to God to bring about repentance (a change of mind) and restoration (bringing the person back into fellowship with God).*

80. GOLDEN APPLES IN SILVER SETTINGS

Like apples of gold in settings of silver is a word spoken in right circumstances.

Proverbs 25:11

Imagine you are close buddies with someone. You share secrets, you laugh together, you make plans—you even share your deepest thoughts. Then you do something that makes you unpopular. And one day your friend tells a group of people that she doesn't even know you. How would you feel? What would you say to her? This is exactly what happened between the Lord Jesus and his close friend and disciple Simon Peter. At one point, Jesus was popular. Crowds of Jewish people shouted, "Hosanna to the Son of David; blessed is He who comes in the name of the Lord" (Matthew 21:9). A short time later, opinions changed. People began to yell out, "Let Him be crucified!" It suddenly became dangerous to be associated with this man from Nazareth, Jesus.

During Jesus' last meal with His disciples, before His betrayal and death, He told them that they would *all* abandon Him that very night. Peter seemed offended. He announced to the whole group, "'Even though all may fall away because of You, I will never fall away.' Jesus said to him, 'Truly I say to you that this very night, before a cock crows, you shall deny Me three times.' Peter said to Him, 'Even if I have to die with You, I will not deny You'" (Matthew 26:33-35).

Of course the Lord Jesus was right. Three different times, Peter denied he even knew his Savior. No sooner had he spoken, than Jesus walked by His frightened disciple. "And the Lord turned and looked at Peter. And Peter remembered the word of the Lord...And he [the disciple] went out and wept bitterly" (Luke 22:61, 62). How heartbreaking for both of them!

Shortly after Jesus' death, burial, and resurrection, Peter went fishing with several of the other disciples. He was probably feeling pretty discouraged, knowing he had denied knowing the Lord of Glory—the very One who died on that cruel wooden cross for him. On top of that, there didn't seem to be a single fish in the lake.

Suddenly, Jesus appeared on the beach roasting fish and bread over a fire. He cheerfully called to the disciples, "Come and have breakfast" (John 21:12). And they went.

You would expect Jesus to be furious with Peter for denying Him, the Creator of the universe. Right after breakfast, Jesus speaks to Peter who was probably sitting off to the side, quite embarrassed. Instead of bringing up the past, Jesus talked to his disciple about the present and the future. Three times He asks Peter if he loves Him, and each time Peter confesses that he does. Then Jesus urges the big fisherman to devote the rest of his life to feeding God's flock—helping other believers grow strong in their faith.

This is what a word spoken in the right circumstances is like. When kind and loving words are spoken at the right time, they are very valuable. Today's verse compares them to precious gold set in silver.

WHAT DO YOU THINK?

1. Can you think of a time when someone you thought was a trusted and loyal friend, suddenly started acting like he or she didn't even know you? How did you feel? Were you angry or sad? Did you want to get back at them?

2. Why do you think Peter was so certain that he would never deny that he knew Jesus? Do you think he really understood his own heart and mind? What was he forgetting?

3. What do you learn about Jesus' character in the way He responded to Peter on the beach?

ANSWERS TO YOUR QUESTIONS

1. *This is a personal opinion. You could ask each child present and also share your own experience.*

2. *Peter's pride got the best of him, and he seemed to be thinking that he was stronger and more loyal than he really was. Jeremiah 17:9 says, "The heart is more deceitful than all else and is desperately sick; who can understand it?" Peter was forgetting that strength and courage come from walking with the Lord.*

3. *That Jesus is forgiving and does not hold grudges; that Jesus always wants to build people up and not tear them down; that Jesus wants to meet our physical needs (the fish and bread) as well as our spiritual needs; and that Jesus understands the importance of a "word spoken in right circumstances."*

81. CHECK OUT YOUR HEROES!

Like clouds and wind without rain is a man who boasts of his gifts falsely.

Proverbs 25:14

On January 29, 1992, a huge ocean-going ship heading from Hong Kong to the USA lost three containers in a storm in the Pacific Ocean. Guess what was in those containers. Almost 30,000 plastic bathtub toys!

Imagine this little fleet of ducks, frogs, and turtles bobbing along on the ocean currents. They floated north past Japan, around the west coast of Alaska, and into the Arctic Ocean. Like a miniature parade, the toys continued across the Bering Strait and then southward down the coast of Greenland. Eager children, who had followed the progress of these sturdy toys for years, discovered battered plastic frogs and ducks along the east coast beaches of the USA and across the Atlantic in Britain.

One of the most remarkable aspects of this story is that this trip took fifteen years. You can imagine the storms and icebergs they experienced. Probably some whales gobbled a few of them down, only to bring them up just as fast. They were even frozen in place in the Arctic for *four years*. When the sun finally freed them, they continued on their danger-filled trip. By the time they had finished their voyage, some had travelled 17,000 miles.

What is the lesson for us in this story? These little plastic animals captured the imaginations of children on several continents. They had braved the worst weather on earth and completed their journey scraped and blistered. We can say they are just hunks of plastic, but I'm sure to a lot of children, these make-believe ducks and turtles were heroes. They couldn't brag about themselves. But who doesn't admire them? [7]

Today's verse talks about people who brag on their own gifts and abilities. Have you ever seen big black clouds roll overhead; sometimes with wind gusts and the odd flash of lightning? You think, "O boy! We're in for a rainstorm." But the clouds pass over without letting go a single drop of rain—they don't amount to anything. They even look like rain clouds, but at the appropriate time they don't produce any showers.

That's what a braggart is like. Rarely do people like to hear someone boast about how smart they are, or what a great athlete they are, or even how many good things they have done for other people. We don't have to brag on ourselves. It's just our pride wanting to express itself, and we know how God feels about pride.

Let other people brag on you if they want. When you choose to live in obedience to Jesus Christ and His Word, He will see to it that other people notice you. And it will be the Lord Jesus in you who receives the glory (see 1 Peter 5:6). That's the kind of hero you want to be.

WHAT DO YOU THINK?

1. What countries did the plastic toys pass on their long 17,000 mile trip? How long did the trip take? Try to trace the trip on a world map.

2. Some people constantly brag about how smart, how strong, or how popular they are. Why do you think they do that?

3. Why is it not necessary for Christians to brag on themselves? How does God feel about us bragging?

ANSWERS TO YOUR QUESTIONS

1. *China, Japan, USA (Alaska), Russia, Arctic Canada, Greenland, the United Kingdom (England, Ireland, Scotland, and Wales), USA (eastern coastline). Some probably even floated as far south as Central and South America and Africa. The trip took 15 years.*

2. *Personal opinion. People who brag a lot are trying to impress other people about their own greatness. When we have Jesus Christ in our life, we want to brag about Him.*

3. *James 1:17 says that everything good and profitable about us comes from God. Since that's the case, why would we brag about these qualities, when we have received them as gifts from our loving heavenly Father? Today's verse makes it clear how God feels about braggarts—they're like empty clouds without rain in them. They don't do anyone any good.*

82. FAITHFUL LIKE A TOOTHACHE AND A SPRAINED ANKLE

Like a bad tooth and an unsteady foot is confidence in a faithless man in time of trouble.

Proverbs 25:19

Have you ever had a toothache that hurt like crazy? How about a broken toe or a sprained ankle? Do you remember how hard it was to put any weight on it? I'm sure, the pain was no fun.

What a great picture, though, of a person who is totally unreliable. They just are a constant pain. You never know when they will find a new way to let you down and disappoint you.

Elisha was an Old Testament prophet who lived in Israel about 500 years before Jesus was born on earth. He faithfully trusted God, and so the Lord worked many mighty miracles through him. This godly man had a servant named Gehazi, who would travel with the prophet. He would probably take care of things like meals, travel arrangements (either a camel or a donkey—not a train or plane), and clean clothes. What a privilege Gehazi had to learn about God from his master. But did he?

One day, Elisha heals the leprosy of Naaman, a very powerful captain of the army of the King of Aram—a neighboring Gentile nation. Naaman was expecting Elisha to heal him through some great ceremony. After all, he was a mighty warrior and a VIP (very important person). When Naaman pulls up in front of Elisha's house in his chariot, the prophet does not greet him. Instead he sends a messenger to tell Naaman to go and wash seven times in the muddy Jordan River and his disease would be cured. Yuk! Although the captain was angry and disappointed, he reluctantly followed the prophet's orders. And guess what—he was totally healed.

Re-enter Gehazi, Elisha's servant! He knows that Naaman had offered a reward to his master for the healing miracle; and he is disappointed that Elisha didn't accept it. He sees an opportunity to get some money for himself, so he chases after Naaman. He lies to the army captain and tells him that Elisha has changed his mind and will accept some silver and other valuables after all.

Naaman is so thankful to be healed of leprosy that he gladly gives Gehazi even more than he requests. So, Elisha's servant stores the loot in his house and returns to his master just like nothing happened—except for one small detail. God knew all about it, and He informed Elisha. We read, "But he [Gehazi] went in and stood before his master. And Elisha said to him, 'Where have you been, Gehazi?' And he said, 'Your servant went nowhere.' Then he [Elisha] said to him, 'Did not my heart go with you, when the man [Naaman] turned from his chariot to meet you? Is it a time to receive money...? Therefore, the leprosy of Naaman shall cleave to you and to your descendants forever.' So he [Gehazi] went out from his presence a leper as white as snow" (2 Kings 5:25-27).

What a lesson! Gehazi let his master down. He also caused himself and his descendants great pain. If being a faithless man is like a toothache or a sprained ankle, doesn't it make you want to obey the Lord and have Him call you "faithful"?

WHAT DO YOU THINK?

1. Why was Naaman, the army captain, insulted when he arrived at the prophet Elisha's house to receive treatment for his leprosy?

2. Gehazi would never be rich working as Elisha's servant. What advantage did he have of being with God's prophet all the time?

3. In what ways was Gehazi like a toothache or a sprained ankle?

ANSWERS TO YOUR QUESTIONS

1. *Elisha never even came out of his house to talk to him, but sent a messenger to tell him to go and dunk himself in the muddy Jordan River seven times. God undoubtedly told Elisha to do this, because Naaman was a proud man. Naaman expected Elisha to meet him in person, call on his God, and wave his hand over the diseased area to heal him.*

2. *Gehazi had a wonderful opportunity to see God work in miraculous ways through his master; to talk with Elisha about the close friendship his master had with God; and most of all, to learn how to enjoy a closeness with God himself.*

3. *As a result of God healing Naaman, the army captain admitted that there was no true god in all the earth except the God of Israel. For Gehazi to deceive him with lies that Elisha had changed his mind and now wanted payment, not only made Elisha look bad, but also Elisha's God. Gehazi was a terrible testimony for God.*

83. WHY BE FOOLISH WITH A FOOL?

Do not answer a fool according to his folly, lest you also be like him. Answer a fool as his folly deserves, lest he be wise in his own eyes.

Proverbs 26:4, 5

When I first met Brad, he was only three days away from entering military training in the US Air Force. He had loving parents and great opportunities ahead of him. He and I met in an unusual manner.

I was chairman of the New Tribes Bible Institute at the time. Someone had broken into our school garage and stolen things. So we had several male students take turns watching the garage at night from a hidden location, to try to identify the culprit.

One night about one a.m., the phone startled me from a sound sleep. The men on guard had seen two figures enter the garage, and they were still inside. I quickly called other staff men to meet me by the garage, asked my wife to phone the police, and looked around for a baseball bat. Why is it that at a time like that, all you can find in the dark is a beach ball?

We could hear the robbers stomping around inside the garage, especially when they stepped on something metal. Suddenly the garage door flew up and two figures bolted out the door, fleeing in opposite directions. As one dark figure darted past me, I took off after him with a student named Bob. Around the building we tore and raced down the sloping lawn in front of the school. I could feel the blood throbbing in my temples, and in my mind a mixture of dread and anger. Bob and I were foolish to chase the robber, but at a time like that your emotions overrule your common sense.

As we charged down the front lawn towards the street, Bob and I fanned out in order to cut off the robber's escape. The dark form in front of us angled towards me. I wasn't even sure what I would do if I caught up to him. My only thought was that we had to put an end to the robberies. We ran across the empty street ahead of us, and I followed the figure into a restaurant parking lot. I grabbed him by the jacket and mumbled some threats for him not to move. I took his wallet and flipped it over to Bob who had joined us by now. We would at least have his identification in case he escaped. Within a few minutes the police arrived and took Brad away.

Several days later, we visited the young man's parents. Until his arrest, they had no idea their son was sneaking out his bedroom window and stealing. Some of the Bible Institute men met with Brad, and he claimed he trusted in Christ. But he even stole from the students' dorm rooms. Of course the Air Force did not accept him. His stupidity cost him dearly.

We don't like to call anyone a *fool*, but God has done that for us. One of today's verses says to "answer a fool as his folly [unwise choices] deserves." That may mean that we have to say in a kind but firm way, "Sorry, I can't continue this discussion. It wouldn't be wise."

WHAT DO YOU THINK?

1. Why do you think that the Brad in our story qualified as a fool?

2. Today's verse says that Christians should not answer a foolish person "according to his folly." What do you think that means?

3. How do you think a Christian should answer a foolish person "as his folly deserves"?

ANSWERS TO YOUR QUESTIONS

1. *Brad had parents who loved him, and he had already been accepted into the military. Yet, he still chose to break into buildings just three days before appearing for training. He did a poor job of choosing friends—he hung out with a law breaker. Brad didn't learn from his mistakes. He foolishly broke into the same building several times in the same week.*

2. *People who choose to be foolish because of their sin, tend to think and reason foolishly. It's useless to enter into a discussion with such a person, because we would have to think like they do. Ephesians 4:15 says that we should speak the truth in love. That's still the best formula.*

3. *We should not be offensive, harsh, critical, or unloving. Instead, we should be honest with them in a kind but firm way. Don't be drawn into a "foolish discussion," but be truthful. Then leave God's truth to work away on the foolish person's heart.*

84. DON'T BE LIKE THE THREE-TOED SLOTH!

The sluggard [lazy person] buries his hand in the dish; he is weary of bringing it to his mouth again. The sluggard is wiser in his own eyes than seven men who can give a discreet answer.
Proverbs 26:15, 16

One of the funniest looking animals on God's green earth is the three-toed sloth. It almost looks like it was made from left-over body parts. The sloth's head looks too small for its body, and its great long arms appear to be made for a larger animal.

The most interesting characteristic of the sloth is how it moves—in slow motion. It looks a little like an ugly monkey, so you expect it to be jumping all over excitedly like monkeys do. But the sloth is in no hurry to get where it's going. Its name has even come to be associated with people who choose to be lazy. You wouldn't exactly call the sloth a celebrity animal.

Another unusual aspect of the sloth is that they have three long claws on each foot. This allows them to climb trees, but hinders them on the ground. So they spend most of their entire life in trees, often hanging upside down. Sloths don't care about personal hygiene either. Green algae [microscopic plants] often grow on them—not great for body odor, but helpful for hiding in the trees.

The funniest feature of this gray-haired, long-legged creature is its undersized skull. On its little round head is a yellow face with black, sad looking eyes. Its mouth, however, seems to wear a constant silly grin. Our creator God sure has a sense of humor.[8]

The sluggard in today's verse refers to someone who chooses to be slothful or lazy—so lazy, in fact, that he can't even lift his food from the plate up to his mouth. Hopefully, by the time he missed a few meals, he would get over that problem.

Jesus also had something to say about slothfulness. One day He told a parable (a story that teaches truth) about a wealthy man who went on a trip. Before he left, he gave five talents of silver to one of his slaves, two to the next, and one to the last. The slave who received the five talents invested his money, and he was able to double it to ten. His fellow slave with two talents earned two

205

more by hard work and good decisions. But the guy with the one talent feared his master and buried it in the ground.

The slaves' master returned and very quickly called for the slaves to report on what they had done with their gifts. When he heard how the slave with five talents had doubled his money, he praised him and gave him a reward saying, "Well done, good and faithful slave; you were faithful with a few things, I will put you in charge of many things, enter into the joy of your master" (Matthew 25:21). Similarly, the master rewarded the slave who received two talents, and doubled the amount with his wise choices. But he stopped smiling when he heard the last slave's report. How foolish to bury a gift instead of using it.

God has given you and me skills and abilities unique to us. He wants us to work hard during our lives to expand those skills. If laziness isn't bad enough, the man in today's verses thinks he's smarter than seven wise men. I don't want to live like a sluggard—or like a three-toed sloth either.

WHAT DO YOU THINK?

1. Describe a three-toed sloth. What does it mean to be slothful?

2. How much did the master in Jesus' parable give to each of the three slaves? What was it that impressed the master about the behavior of the first two slaves, while he was away?

3. The slave given one talent buried his money in the ground because he feared his master and didn't want to lose the talent. What's so wrong with that? At least he didn't spend it!

206

ANSWERS TO YOUR QUESTIONS

1. *About the size of a small dog*
   Covered in long gray hair—sometimes green with algae
   Three long claws on each foot
   Lives in trees; has trouble walking on the ground
   Their head seems too small for their body
   A yellow face, large black eyes, and a constant grin
   Hangs upside down on tree branches
   To be slothful is to be lazy and slow moving

2. *The master gave away 5, 2, and 1 talents to three of his slaves. The first two slaves worked hard to see how they could invest their money wisely, so that it would earn interest.*

3. *The point is that this slave did nothing with his gift. God creates each of us as unique individuals, but He also gives us gifts and skills. He wants us to develop those skilled areas by working hard in His service as well as in serving one another. If we do, we will bear fruit for His glory. If we refuse to, but just keep our gifts for ourselves, we are selfish and of little benefit to others.*

85. HOW ABOUT TOMORROW?

Do not boast about tomorrow, for you do not know what a day may bring forth.

Proverbs 27:1

Have you ever wished you could turn your TV to the *Tomorrow Channel* and watch what your next day will be like? Would you like to check out what you'll look like at your high school graduation? At times I have looked at a photo of my wife and children, and thought how fun it would have been to see that picture when I was in college.

Of course, it would be great to see ahead when events are happy ones. But what about tragedies? Could we still live happy, carefree lives if we knew we might be helpless to deal with some disaster? Probably not. But if Jesus was right here in a physical body, right now, and we could ask Him one question, I think most of us would ask about the years ahead of us. Maybe God is being kind to us by not revealing our tomorrows to us today.

Christ's disciples were no different than we are—James and John even asked Jesus to rearrange the future for their benefit: "'Teacher, we want You to do for us whatever we ask of You.' And He said to them, 'What do you want Me to do for you?' And they said to Him, 'Grant that we may sit in Your glory [in heaven], one on Your right, and one on Your left'" (Mark 10:35-37).

Even after Jesus rose from the dead and was preparing to return to His heavenly Father, the disciples still asked Him about the future. Let's listen in! "And so when they had come together, they were asking Him, saying, 'Lord, is it at this time You are restoring the kingdom to Israel?' He said to them, 'It is not for you to know times…which the Father has fixed by His own authority'" (Acts 1:6, 7).

So, it sounds like the Lord just wants us to leave the future to Him. It's better that we learn to trust His loving heart, believing that He knows what is the very best for us. Imagine the mess we'd probably make if we were in charge of our own futures.

On the other hand, God has given us some clues in His Word about the future—just enough to give us hope. Here are a few exciting highlights we can look forward to:

1. We will be present with Jesus the moment we pass away. (2 Corinthians 5:8)
2. God will give us an eternal body that will be just like Jesus. (I John 3:2)
3. We will see friends and relatives again in heaven who passed away before us.
4. We will see heaven itself; more beautiful than anything we've ever seen. (Revelation 21:10-27)
5. There will be no more death, sadness, crying, pain, or sickness. (Revelation 21:4)

What a wise heavenly Father we have! He doesn't burden our minds with anxious thoughts of the future. Instead, he gives us enough details about eternal life with Him to keep our hope alive.

WHAT DO YOU THINK?

1. Have you ever wished that you could see yourself at some point in the future? If you could choose one future time period, which would it be and why?

2. There are people called *psychics* (fortune tellers) who claim they can tell you true things about your future using tea leaves, playing cards, and the stars. Why do we know that this is a false claim?

3. Jesus said to His disciples, "It is not for you to know times...which the Father has fixed by His own authority" (Acts 1:7). Explain that verse in your own words.

ANSWERS TO YOUR QUESTIONS

1. *Personal opinion. You may want to ask each child.*

2. *Only God knows exactly what will happen in our remaining years on earth. People who claim to know the future are not telling the truth. God tells us a few things in His Word that will happen as a part of His divine will. Because He alone knows what the future will bring, we are totally dependent on Him.*

3. *It is not in the Father's plan to reveal our futures to us. God has total authority over what will happen. However, He does give us some details in His Word about what will happen at the end of the world and in heaven.*

86. LOVING ENOUGH TO BE HONEST

Better is open rebuke than love that is concealed. Faithful are the wounds of a friend, but deceitful are the kisses of an enemy.
Proverbs 27:5, 6

What are the "wounds of a friend" that today's verse talks about? When our family was in missionary training, the men would play touch football after work was finished and before supper. After one of our games, one player—who also happened to be a staff member—asked if he could talk to me alone. We played on the same team and he was the quarterback, while I was a receiver. We found some shade on the corner of the playing field, and he began to share his thoughts with me.

"Can I share an observation with you from our football game?" When I nodded, he began to describe in a kind but honest way, a consistent pattern he saw in my playing. Looking me in the eyes, he said, "I've noticed that when I call a long pass play, you run down the right side lines, and if my throw is slightly beyond you, you don't make much of an effort to go after it. I know this is only a football game, but it can also demonstrate our attitude toward life and work. When you become a missionary, will you quit when the going gets rough? If you are taking supplies to a tribal missionary by boat, and you run into a few rapids, will you turn back? Or will you keep pressing on until you finish the job?"

At first I felt like I had let him and the team down. Really I just had hurt feelings. I respected this man and didn't want to disappoint him. As I thought and prayed about his comments, I could begin to see that what my friend was saying to me was true. I remembered a parent/teacher conference when I was in fifth grade. My parents had come home with this report: "He knows his work, but he doesn't really give of himself. He will work up to a certain point and then quit—he doesn't push himself beyond that."

Now, as a young man training to be a missionary, I still had that "quitter attitude." I was willing to float along and not exert myself. Thankfully, my friend cared enough to tell me the truth in a kind and respectful way. And so I asked God to help me to change. I still have good memories of the faithful man who "wounded" me in a loving way.

The second half of today's verse talks about the "kisses of an enemy." What are the kisses and who is the enemy? When a person calls herself your friend, when she knows you are heading down a dangerous road with your words and actions, and she fails to be honest with you in a kind and loving way, is she really a true friend?

For sure, it can be hard to talk with a close friend about a serious need you see in her life. She may feel wounded at first. But when you ask the Lord for the right words and you go with a kind attitude, you can both benefit. Anyone can flatter someone, but only a true friend will tell you the truth. Are you that kind of friend?

WHAT DO YOU THINK?

1. What does the "wounds of a friend" mean? What are the "kisses of an enemy"?

2. I could have responded to my staff friend by saying, "You are just being critical of me? You are the one who really has the problem. You throw the ball too far and then blame it on me." Would that have been a good response? Why or why not?

3. John 15:13 says, "Greater love has no one than this, that one lay down his life for his friends." How would this verse apply to today's lesson?

ANSWERS TO YOUR QUESTIONS

1. *When a good friend tells you honestly about something he sees in your life that could be harmful to you if you don't change it—such as anger or dishonesty—it can hurt your feelings at first. These are called the "wounds of a friend," not because they are bad, but the truth often hurts. If you are willing to admit that area to God and let Him show you more clearly, He will make it a positive experience for you. The "kisses of an enemy" come from people who constantly tell you how great and wonderful you are, even when you do things that are wrong. They are not being a help to you.*

2. *If I had brushed my friend's comments aside with a lot of excuses, I would have been closing my heart to God's Word where we're told, "Whatever you do, do your work heartily, as for the Lord rather than for men" (Colossians 3:23). My weakness of giving up rather than trying my hardest would only have gotten worse.*

3. *There is always a danger of losing a friend when you are completely honest with him. When a person loves you enough to tell you the truth—even when it might hurt a little—he is a true friend who is willing to risk even your anger in order to see you helped.*

87. THE TEN COMMANDMENTS OF GOOD WORKERS

He who tends the fig tree will eat its fruit; and he who cares for his master will be honored.
Proverbs 27:18

I launched my working career at the ripe old age of five. The pay wasn't all that great—a couple of cookies, some jelly beans, or a few pennies. On garbage collection day, I waited until the truck went by; then I would carry the neighbors' empty garbage containers up to their door. Even at five, I knew enough to rattle the cans so the householder was aware of how generous I was being with my time.

I could hardly wait until I reached middle school age to deliver newspapers. It did limit me being able to play some sports, but I enjoyed having some of my own money. After a couple of years in "the newspaper business," I graduated to being a delivery boy for a drug store.

During the summers of my high school years, I worked as a chore boy at a resort in northern Ontario, Canada. I did everything from cutting grass to drying dishes. Proverbs 14:23 says, "In all labor there is profit, but mere talk leads only to poverty." I believe our heavenly Father would rather we be hard workers than just good talkers.

You may already have babysat or raked leaves for a neighbor, so you know a little about working for pay. Here are ten principles to keep in mind for now; they'll also help you when you become a working adult. I call them, *The Ten Commandments of Good Workers:*

1. Arrive at work a little earlier than you are required; stay until the job is done, or your boss or employer says you can go.
2. Be alert when your boss gives instructions on how he wants the job done. Listening is very important in order to do your work his way and not yours.
3. Do more than is asked of you, not less. Not only is it a good Christian testimony, but it makes the boss want to keep you on as a worker.

214

4. When at work, your time is your employer's, not yours. Workers who stand around talking are costing their boss money.
5. Be honest! If you break something, tell your boss about it right away.
6. Respect your employer. Even if your boss is friendly, keep your relationship on an employer/employee basis.
7. Be thankful for your job! Many people can't find work.
8. Be dependable, so your boss can rely on your word. If you can't make it to work or you're going to be late, call your boss well ahead of time to let him know.
9. Be a learner! By being willing to learn new skills, you are making yourself more valuable to your employer.
10. Be a testimony for Jesus Christ! You may be the only Christian your boss knows.

Here is one more helpful verse: "Whatever you do, do your work heartily, as for the Lord rather than for men; knowing that from the Lord you will receive the reward of the inheritance. *It is the Lord Christ whom you serve"* (Colossians 3:23, 24).

WHAT DO YOU THINK?

1. Explain in your own words what Proverbs 14:23 means: "In all labor there is profit, but mere talk leads only to poverty."

2. Why should we do even more than our employer requires of us?

3. Why is being dependable and keeping your word so important to being a good employee?

ANSWERS TO YOUR QUESTIONS

1. *Working hard at an honest job is good for us. It teaches us skills, it develops our minds and bodies, and provides money for our needs. Those who prefer to just stand around and talk will have trouble finding work and so will constantly be poor. By doing nothing on the job, you are proving to your boss that you're not needed.*

2. *It is a rare quality for an employee to do even more than a job requires. Besides making that worker valuable to their boss, it is a testimony to the generosity of Christ.*

3. *You may be the only Christian your employer knows. If you are unreliable and you constantly break your word, your boss could also look at Christianity the same way. By keeping your word, you are declaring that God keeps His word also, since you are one of His children.*

88. TO BE BOLD AS A LION

The wicked flee when no one is pursuing, but the righteous are bold as a lion.
Proverbs 28:1

Why are some people bold and courageous, while others are fearful to try anything new? We should probably start by finding out the meaning of these words. *Bold* and *courageous* mean "fearless, brave, and daring."

The most decorated US hero of World War 2 is a young Texan named Audie Murphy. He joined the US Army at 17 by having his sister change the date on his birth certificate. The Marines and the Navy had refused him for being too small. He joined the invasion of Italy and France as a part of the 3rd Infantry Division. When a German machine gunner killed his best friend, Audie wiped out the entire machine gun crew by himself. Then he turned the enemy's machine gun on several other German positions. For his bravery, he received the Distinguished Service Cross—the second highest honor in the US military. Several weeks later, he received two Silver Stars for other brave deeds.

On January 26, 1945, a bitterly cold day in France, Lt. Audie Murphy sent his few remaining soldiers to the rear. Although wounded in the leg, Audie took over a burning tank's .50 caliber machine gun and held off a full squad of German infantry by himself. Eventually he called up his rag-tag group of 19 soldiers, and together they counter-attacked and drove off the enemy. For this, Audie was awarded the Medal of Honor—the US military's highest honor. By war's end, this courageous hero had received 33 US medals, plus five medals from France and one from Belgium—all by 20 years of age.[9]

When I think of courageous people in the Bible, Jonathan, the son of Israel's King Saul and close friend of David comes to mind. Jonathan decides to attack a Philistine garrison with only his armor bearer to help him—he never even told his father. Where was the king? Sitting under a tree with his 600 soldiers, wondering what to do next.

All of Jonathan's options looked bad at this point—the enemy garrison stood on the top of a sheer cliff and he was at the bottom. If I was going on the attack, I would at least have waited until 3:00 a.m., but not Jonathan! In the light of day, he told his assistant, "Come and let us cross over to the garrison of these [Gentiles]; perhaps the Lord will work for us, for the Lord is not restrained to save by many or by few" (1 Samuel 14:6). And the Lord did save. Jonathan won a great victory over the Philistines that day, with only the help of his armorbearer.

Every courageous person isn't necessarily a Christian, but every Christian should be courageous. Why? Because the same God who helped Jonathan will help us! We are not involved in a physical fight, but we still face powerful enemies every day of our lives. Courage for us may mean speaking up for Jesus when we hear people cursing His name, or by telling the truth when we're tempted to lie. Take those first steps to be courageous by faith. All the forces of heaven are standing by to help you.

WHAT DO YOU THINK?

1. Every courageous person isn't necessarily a Christian, but every Christian should be courageous. Explain why that is true.

2. Why do you think courageous people often make good leaders?

3. Suppose you are asked to do something that is very hard, very important, or even slightly dangerous, and you don't feel very courageous—in fact you are very nervous about it. What would be a couple of wise things to do?

ANSWERS TO YOUR QUESTIONS

1. *Every Christian should be courageous because if we are in God's will, He says that He will be with us. (See Hebrews 13:5)*

2. *Courageous people often make good leaders because they build up courage in their followers by their brave example. People will often feel that a difficult task is impossible to do. If the leader either does it himself, or is able to convince his followers that they can do it also, they develop trust and confidence in their leader.*

3. *The most important step would be to pray about it, and make sure it is something God wants you to do. The Lord is eager to make clear to His children what will please Him. It is also good to ask those you have confidence in—like dad and mom—for their advice. If you have the time before you have to decide, think about the short-term and long-term results. Ask yourself, "Will this decision glorify God, or am I thinking only about myself?"*

89. WHAT YOU SEE IS NOT ALWAYS WHAT YOU GET

Better is the poor who walks in his integrity, than he who is crooked though he be rich.
Proverbs 28:6

Sometimes our eyes can trick us. What we think we are seeing isn't really the true picture. Artist Bev Doolittle paints pictures of animals, landscapes, and Indians. In some of them she likes to hide animals in the background that you miss at first glance. For example, in one painting called *Pintos*[10], you easily see a landscape of melting snow. But as you continue to look you begin to notice a group of pinto Indian ponies standing together on the hillside of snow and rock. Later you wonder how you missed them.

Life can be like that too. A man may be well-dressed and driving an expensive car. People call him "Sir" and open his car door for him. But in reality, he is a gangster and a threat to society. Or we may see a young woman with no makeup and frizzy hair—we think she is probably homeless. The truth is, she's an oral surgeon who treats children with cleft palates for free in a third world country.

Picture Jesus as He walked the dusty roads of Judea, 2000 years ago. He is God and the Creator of the entire universe, but He owned almost nothing. He didn't even have a place to lay His head at night or a donkey to ride on. He earned no salary and depended on the kindness of others for His meals.

One evening, probably as He was preparing to sleep on a bench or maybe in an alley, a wealthy man named Nicodemus approached him. This expensively dressed man greeted Jesus and stated that He must have God with Him because of His miracles. The Lord wasted no time in telling Nicodemus what he needed: "Truly, truly, I say to you, unless one is born again, he cannot see the kingdom of God" (John 3:3).

What a contrast! God's glorious Son, who had no earthly home, offered eternal life to this wealthy Pharisee who was sneakily looking for Jesus in the dark, so his religious buddies wouldn't see him. Nicodemus may have trusted in Christ that night or soon after. John 19:39 mentions how Nicodemus, along with Joseph, claimed Christ's body after the crucifixion, wrapped it in linen with spices, and placed Him in a tomb.

One lesson we can learn from this story is that integrity (or a reputation of truthfulness) is far more valuable than all the wealth in the world—just like today's verse says.

WHAT DO YOU THINK?

1. Have you ever looked at something and found out later it was altogether different than what you thought you saw? Explain, please.

2. Why do you think we tend to give more respect to wealthy people (even if they're evil) than we do to poor people?

3. Read James 2:1-9, please. Try to explain these verses in your own words.

ANSWERS TO YOUR QUESTIONS

1. *Personal opinion. You may want to ask each child.*

2. *In our culture, wealthy people are often treated with more respect than poor people are, without even getting to know either one. Both attitudes are wrong and not how Jesus looked at people.*

3. *Personal opinion.*

90. WHEN THE PRODIGAL SON COMES HOME

He who conceals his transgressions will not prosper, but he who confesses and forsakes them will find compassion.
Proverbs 28:13

One of the tenderest stories in the Bible of a father's love for his rebellious child is commonly called *The Prodigal Son*, which means the wayward son. The beauty of this story that Jesus told to the Pharisees and scribes as they grumbled about the Lord eating with sinners, is that the father in the story represents God the Father. The rebellious son pictures all Christians who walk away from His will.

The son, we'll call him Junior, demands his inheritance from his dad. He's wrong to do this—normally an inheritance is only received after the parents die. But his father graciously gives it to him. Junior can't wait to get to the big city for what he thinks will be a "good time." The Bible says that he "squandered [wasted] his estate with loose living" (Luke 15:13b). He blows every last cent on things and people who toss him aside when his funds run out.

Now, the only job he can find is tromping around in a field feeding pigs. He can't even afford a meal, so he eats the same food as the pigs are eating, "and no one was giving anything to him" (Luke 15:16b). What a picture this is of a Christian trying to find joy and fulfillment in a world without Christ.

When Junior finally realizes that he isn't living any better than the pigs, he admits his foolishness to himself and decides to return home to beg his father for forgiveness. *I'll be so glad to just be a servant in my dad's house,* he thinks. *I'm no longer worthy to be called a son.* So he leaves the pigs snorting in the field and heads for home.

The high point of the story is in verse 20: "But while he was still a long way off, his father saw him [Dad must have been constantly looking down the road for his son's return], and felt compassion for him, and ran and embraced him, and kissed him."

Instead of telling Junior, "You're a fool," or lecturing him, the father forgives him. What a great picture of our heavenly

Father! He doesn't want us punishing ourselves—He only asks us to repent or change our minds about our sin and admit it truthfully to Him. In response, just like the father in the story, He has compassion on us, He runs and embraces us, and kisses us— all spiritually speaking of course—forgives our sin, and calls us *son* or *daughter.*

What a wonderful heavenly Father we Christians have! He loves us so much and He longs to have a close family relationship with us.

WHAT DO YOU THINK?

1. In the story Jesus told of the Prodigal Son, who did the son represent? Who did the father picture?

2. How would you describe what took place in Junior's heart when he realized he was eating the same food as the pigs?

3. Describe God's attitude when His children sin and then repent or admit their wrong truthfully to Him.

ANSWERS TO YOUR QUESTIONS

1. *The Prodigal Son represents all Christian men, women, and children when they sin. The father is a picture of God the Father. God does not call Himself "Father," nor does He call people His "children" until they are born spiritually into His family.*

2. *The Bible says that he "came to his senses." That means that he admitted to himself that he had done wrong for a lot of reasons. He could then see that he didn't deserve to be called a son, or to have a loving father who had been so generous to him. So, he decides to go and ask his father for forgiveness and experience the joy of the family again.*

3. *Like Junior's father, God is constantly looking for us to return to Him when we sin. He doesn't require that we punish ourselves, or try to pay somehow for having sinned. When we truthfully admit our sin to ourselves and to Him, He "runs" to forgive us. We don't then become a second-level servant until we prove ourselves, but we are forgiven sons and daughters in God's family, just as if we had never sinned.*

91. WHAT DOES ANGER LOOK LIKE?

When a wise man has a controversy [difference of opinion] with a foolish man, the foolish man either rages or laughs, and there is no rest... A fool always loses his temper, but a wise man holds it back.

Proverbs 29:9, 11

Anger. It can snarl, slink away, sneak back, and lash out again. Proverbs contains many verses on this subject. I wonder why that is? Could it possibly be because all of us struggle with anger in one form or another? Looking back over my own life, I can recall a time when I wasn't walking with the Lord, that I lost my temper with friends, my wife, and my children— and even with God. I didn't go into a screaming rage, throw things, or hit people. But my anger was just as ugly to God as anyone else's.

Today's verses mention the foolishness of red-faced rages and deceitful laughter. To help us remember, let's compare the types of anger to animals and their behavior:

1. THE HOWLER MONKEY – In the Panama rain forest, I sometimes heard this type of monkey yelling in a haunting voice, hour after hour. There are people who get angry easily, and although they're not violent, they will argue endlessly. And words can hurt.

2. THE WOLVERINE – Pound for pound, this animal is considered one of the fiercest animals alive. Some people feel they have to hurt someone else when they get angry. Countless families have been permanently damaged by such outbursts.

3. THE HYENA – This animal is often called the "laughing hyena" because its howl sounds like someone laughing. Today's verse says that when some people are angry, they laugh and mock the other person. What a sorry sense of humor that is!

4. THE COYOTE – The coyote is a puny version of the wolf. It scavenges for food, but when its bigger cousin comes along, it quietly slinks away. There are people (me included) who get quiet when they are angry and refuse to talk.

5. THE GRIZZLY – Grizzlies are known for stalking their prey—even humans. I have known people who express their anger by quietly getting even with others.

6. THE DEER – God has given the deer excellent hearing and legs that run swiftly. Some angry people react by escaping from the person or situation they are in, so they can be by themselves.

By now you can see that anger shows itself in a variety of ways. God says, "A fool always loses his temper, but a wise man [or woman, teen, or child] holds it back."

WHAT DO YOU THINK?

1. Why do you think there are so many verses in the Bible that talk about the dangers of anger?

2. Some people close up like a clam when they are angry, while others are loud and like to argue. What are the long term results of both types—to the angry person and to others?

3. We discussed five types of anger (and there are probably more). Is there one that you recognize as being typical of you?

ANSWERS TO YOUR QUESTIONS

1. *All of us are tempted to resort to anger when we don't get our way or feel that someone is talking negatively about us. We can make childish decisions that hurt others when we're angry. God's Word says it's just plain foolish.*

2. *The long term results are probably very similar to both the angry one and to others. Because it's foolish to constantly get angry, any type of anger will ruin friendship, hurt job opportunities, and injure marriages and parent-child relationships.*

3. *Personal opinion. You may want to ask each child and even share about yourself.*

92. WHEN A PLAN COMES TOGETHER

Where there is no vision, the people are unrestrained [or stumble], but happy is he who keeps the law.
Proverbs 29:18

It's good to make plans even when you are young. And the Lord is available to help you make those plans (see Proverbs 3:5, 6).

For example, you might want to study math and science; or maybe English and languages are better for you; or you lean toward business and office studies. The same would apply to your college major and beyond. Today's verse says that people stumble when they don't have a *vision* (or plan). For now, the wisest plan may be for you to want to be known as a Christian at school, rather than having no plan at all and letting circumstances decide for you.

I love the story of Joshua preparing to lead the nation of Israel across the Jordan River into the Promised Land. It didn't just happen. God gave Joshua a detailed plan of how and when He wanted His people to cross over. The people were not to move until the priests had entered the river carrying the ark of the covenant—a very special piece of furniture that was important to Israel's worship of God. The priests were to step into the Jordan and stand still.

This was a great step of faith for the priests and the Jewish people. If the Lord did not cause the river to divide, as He had with Moses and the Red Sea, it would be a terrible drowning disaster for everyone. It was important that they follow God's plan. Joshua explained, "that you may know the way by which you shall go, for you have not passed this way before" (Joshua 3:4b).

When God gave the order through Joshua, the priests carrying the ark headed toward the Jordan. The Bible records the event: "And when those who carried the ark came into the Jordan, and the feet of the priests carrying the ark were dipped in the edge of the water (for the Jordan overflows all its banks all the days of harvest), that the waters…rose up in one heap…And the priests

228

who carried the ark of the covenant of the Lord stood firm on dry ground in the middle of the Jordan while all Israel crossed on dry ground..." (Joshua 3:15-17). Everyone followed the plan!

What an exciting time it must have been for Israel to come up out of the river bed onto the firm ground of the Promised Land—forty years after starting out from Egypt. Wouldn't you like to have God help you with your plans? If He can part the waters of a sea and a river, surely He can bring success to your plans.

WHAT DO YOU THINK?

1. To never bother to make plans for what you are doing now and in the future, is a little like driving up to a stop-light and not knowing which road to take. Have you ever thought about making plans for yourself—even about the kinds of friends you would like to have?

2. Have you thought about how you are "known" in your world—at school, with your friends, or your teammates on a sports team? Have you made any "plans" in advance for letting it be known you are a Christian, do you want to blend in, or are you just "letting life happen"?

3. Why do you think God wanted the priests carrying the ark to actually step into the river before He caused it to divide? How would this principle apply to your life?

ANSWERS TO YOUR QUESTIONS

1. *Personal opinion. You may want to ask each child.*

2. *Personal opinion. You may want to ask each child. You could also ask your children for ideas on how to model the Christian life "in their world" by making wise choices and being kind and caring to others.*

3. *God wanted the priests and the people of Israel to trust Him. They had to step into the trial by faith, trusting that God would care for them. The same is true for Christians. God often urges us to step into a situation by faith, before He will visibly work out all the details.*

93. TWO BRAVE WOMEN WHO SAVED THE DAY

A man's pride will bring him low, but a humble spirit will obtain honor.

Proverbs 29:23

Let me introduce you to an amazing woman named Deborah, who lived around the time of Joshua. God raised up judges during these days to point the nation of Israel back to their heavenly Father. These judges often ended up leading the Jewish people into war with the surrounding pagan nations.

At this particular time, Deborah is a judge, and every day sits under a tree in Ephraim, helping her people sort out their difficulties. Their pagan neighbors, the Canaanites, pose a huge problem—especially their king Jabin and his army commander Sisera.

One day, Deborah contacts Barak, a Jewish man, and passes on a message that God has given her. She tells Barak to gather an army of ten thousand men from two Jewish tribes and go to Mount Tabor. God added, "And I will draw out to you Sisera, the commander of Jabin's army, with his chariots [900 of them] and his many troops to the river Kishon; and I will give him into your hand" (Judges 4:7).

How about that? God promises victory even before the battle begins. Do you think Barak trusted God and jumped right into the fight? No! "Then Barak said to her [Deborah], 'If you will go with me, then I will go; but if you will not go with me, I will not go'" (Judges 4:8). What? He's not sure that God's powerful help is enough. He wants Deborah close by before he will go into battle. Deborah rebukes the timid Barak and tells him that she will go with him, but he will not receive any honor for the victory over the Canaanites. A woman will kill Sisera.

Deborah humbly trusts in God and gives the battle cry: "Arise! For this is the day in which the Lord has given Sisera into your hands; behold, the Lord has gone out before you" (Judges 4:14). And God did just as He said—He overpowered the Canaanite army, and the Bible says, "And all the army of Sisera fell by the edge of the sword; not even one was left" (verse 16).

Well, there was one person left—the commander, Sisera. He takes off running for the hills by himself and unfortunately seeks refuge in the house of another brave woman—Jael. The details of how Jael managed to kill this army commander are a little gruesome, but you sure have to admire her boldness and courage (Read Judges 4:17-22). God even destroys Jabin, king of Canaan, because he dared attack Israel.

What lesson can we learn? Our heavenly Father loves a humble attitude and hates pride. When we're humble, we'll depend on God for His help. But pride blinds our eyes; all we see is "the big ME." The apostle Peter reminds us: "And all of you, clothe yourselves with humility toward one another, for God is opposed to the proud, but gives grace to the humble. Humble yourselves, therefore, under the mighty hand of God, that He may exalt you at the proper time, casting all your anxiety upon Him, because He cares for you" (1 Peter 5:5b-7).

I know which side I want to be on!

WHAT DO YOU THINK?

1. What is the main difference between Deborah's attitude and Barak's attitude regarding going to war?

2. Sisera, commander of Canaan's army, caused Barak to be fearful. Why?

3. When God shows us clearly that He wants us to do something, we all experience some level of fear. What would be a good "battle plan" when we experience that fear?

ANSWERS TO YOUR QUESTIONS

1. *When God spoke to Deborah and told her to ask Barak to lead Israel's army against the Canaanites, she believed God and obeyed Him. She was confident in their victory. Barak, on the other hand, said he would only go to war if Deborah would go with him. He did not obey God's command. He doubted what God said.*

2. *Sisera was in command of a huge army that included nine hundred chariots. Barak forgot that God is an "army of ONE!" There is no enemy so large that He is not able to overpower them.*

3. *To begin with, we should admit our fears to God. Why pretend those emotions are not there? But that is when we need to claim an appropriate Bible verse and let the Lord strengthen us to do His will.*

94. WRITTEN ON THE WIND

Who has ascended into heaven and descended? Who has gathered the wind in His fists? Who has wrapped the waters in His garment? Who has established all the ends of the earth? What is His name or His son's name? Surely you know!
Proverbs 30:4

Did God ask the questions in today's verse because He didn't know the answers? Of course not! He *is* the answer! But the questions make us think.

A very similar question and answer time occurred between Job and God Himself. During a time of severe testing, when Job lost everything but his wife and three friends, he *demanded* to talk to God about it. He was sure he could defend himself in front of his heavenly Father, and prove that he had done nothing to deserve all his misery. All of a sudden God gave him that opportunity.

But instead of allowing Job to spend hours complaining about all his troubles and defending his innocence, God quizzed Job by asking, "Who is this that darkens counsel [argues] by words without knowledge? Now...I will ask you, and you instruct Me!" (Job 38:2, 3).

God's questions make Job think. Gradually, he realizes how wonderful the true God is. When we're tempted to be anxious or upset with God, or to wonder if He is in control, it's wise to stop and think about these questions too:
1. Where were you when God formed the earth? (38:4)
2. On what type of base does the earth sit? (38:6)
3. Who set the boundaries for all the oceans? (38:8)
4. Have you ever caused the sun to rise in the dawn? (38:12)
5. What is death all about? (38:17)
6. Where does light and darkness come from? (38:19)
7. From where does the snow and hail come? (38:22)
8. How is the east wind formed? (38:24)
9. Can you make lightning and thunder? (38:25)
10. How is rain formed—or ice—or frost? (38:28, 29)
11. Does anyone but God understand all the galaxies? (38:33)

234

12. Can anyone else create the mind and intelligence? (38:36)
13. Who else can feed all of the earth's animals? (38:39)
14. Can you create the strength of a horse or the grace of an eagle? (39:21, 27)

This same all-powerful God, who has no equal, is the same One who sent His Son to earth to die on the cross. He paid our "sin debt" in full.

What a powerful God we have! What a loving Savior He is! Let's love and serve Him with all our heart!

WHAT DO YOU THINK?

1. While Job was suffering, what did he really want to do more than anything?

2. God did not tell Job why He allowed him to suffer. What did He do instead?

3. Why do you think God responded to Job in the way He did?

ANSWERS TO YOUR QUESTIONS

1. *Job wanted to stand before God, look Him in the eye, and ask Him what he had done so wrong that he deserved all of his misery.*

2. *Using countless examples, God reminded Job of His all-powerful, creative ability. He also asked Job if he was capable of doing these things (knowing obviously that he wasn't).*

3. *Job thought he could win an argument with God, but he was wrong. Second, Job thought he was good and righteous, which apart from God is also not possible. Third, Job needed to catch a glimpse of the greatness and power of the One he was trying to stand up to. And finally, the Lord wanted Job to just trust in almighty God instead of trusting in himself.*

95. THE BOOK THAT NEVER GETS OLD

Every word of God is tested; He is a shield to those who take refuge in Him. Do not add to His words lest He reprove [scold] you, and you be proved a liar.

Proverbs 30:5, 6

People who don't love Jesus Christ delight in tearing down God's Word, the Bible. Here are a few of the arguments that have no basis in truth—and why:

1. **The Bible is an outdated book that doesn't provide any help in our computerized world**.
   Answer: Because God is eternal (no beginning or ending) and He never changes, His Holy Spirit has spoken to certain godly people to write down what He wants us to know. His words which make up the Bible are timeless—they never get old. God has made many promises to those who love Him, which will be true until the end of time. One verse that has strengthened me many times is Isaiah 41:10: "Do not fear, for I am with you; do not anxiously look about you, for I am your God. I will strengthen you, surely I will help you, surely I will uphold you with My righteous right hand."

2. **The various books of the Bible were written by different people, so how can they possibly say the same things?**
   Answer: The books of the Bible were written down by dozens of people, but all that is written is consistent—there are no contradictions. God the Holy Spirit is the author, and these men only copied the words down as He dictated His thoughts to them. We read, "But know this first of all, that no prophecy of Scripture is a matter of one's own interpretation, for no prophecy was ever made by an act of human will [or, a person's own opinion], but men moved by the Holy Spirit spoke from God" (2 Peter 1:20, 21).

3. **The Bible is full of errors.**
   Answer: It's interesting that the people who say this, usually don't know what the supposed errors are, but they're just repeating what they heard other people say. The truth is that

236

even though God used various people to contribute to the Bible, what they said does not disagree. There are several occasions where two accounts of something like the same Old Testament war will give different numbers of soldiers. It's interesting how often archeological discoveries will explain very logically why the numbers are different.

No book other than the Bible has ever been able to accurately predict a future event like the Bible has. Here is what a Bible scholar by the name of Dr. Charles Ryrie said about prophecies or predictions just concerning Jesus Christ: "According to the laws of chance, it would require 200 billion earths, populated with four billion people each, to come up with one person whose life could fulfill 100 accurate prophecies without any errors in sequence [order]. Yet the Scriptures record not 100, but over 300 prophecies that were fulfilled in Christ's first coming alone."[11]

WHAT DO YOU THINK?

1. When people tell you that they think the Bible is old-fashioned or outdated, how might you answer them?

2. The Bible was written by many people over a long period of time. Why does it not contradict itself?

3. What is one good proof that the Bible is *not* "full of errors?"

ANSWERS TO YOUR QUESTIONS

1. *God, the author of the Bible, is eternal (no beginning and no end). He also never changes, so His truth never changes. The principles God gives us in His Word are eternal—many relate to the future, and even talk about our eternity in heaven. So, how could it be outdated?*

2. *The specific author of the Bible is God the Holy Spirit. He spoke to the hearts and minds of godly people, encouraging them to write down what He gave them to say. This means that Scripture was "inspired" or "God breathed."*

3. *Around three hundred prophecies/predictions mention that Jesus Christ would come to earth. All of them have been fulfilled (His first coming) or will be fulfilled (when He comes again). The odds of that happening are impossible by man's standards. But God is all-powerful, and what He predicts will happen.*

96. WHAT AMAZES YOU?

There are three things which are too wonderful for me, four which I do not understand: the way of an eagle in the sky, the way of a serpent on a rock, the way of a ship in the middle of the sea, and the way of a man with a maid.
Proverbs 30:18, 19

Agur, the author of today's proverbs, chose four items out of many that amazed him. Let's look more closely at the eagle, the snake, a ship, and true love between a man and a woman.

On a recent boat trip, the guide showed my wife and me a huge eagle's nest in a pine tree. "Eagles often use the same nest year after year," he said. "The mix of mud and branches can grow to a weight of a ton or more." Four young eagles, still dressed in their brownish-grey feathers, clung to nearby branches. Their head feathers had not yet turned white, so they looked like monks waiting for a church service to begin.

Snakes do not have legs, but they can sure slither quickly. Simply by contracting and relaxing certain muscles at lightning speed, they can travel on land, swim, climb trees, and propel themselves short distances in the air. I remember hiking on the Bruce Trail in Ontario, Canada. Just as we came over a rise in the trail, we experienced a mixture of shock and fear. There was a highly venomous Massasauga rattlesnake, sunning himself in the middle of the path. Yes, we gave him the right-of-way.

What huge metal container over 3 ½ football fields long, can carry up to 5600 people and 85 airplanes, weigh in at a trim 164 million pounds, float in the middle of the ocean, and handle the worst of storms? The US aircraft carrier *John F. Kennedy* can. If Augur was amazed that a small fishing boat could float, he would be flabbergasted at this floating US military city, which cost a mere $4.5 billion.[12]

Because God *is* love and all true love comes from Him, it's wonderful to see Him bring a Christian man and woman together to form a family. It begins with attraction, which leads to romance, as they get to know each other. The young man and woman seek the Lord's direction, and may decide to spend the rest of their lives together. So they plan their wedding. Almighty God is the author of love and marriage—why not let the "Divine Matchmaker" be in charge of the whole relationship?

There are many things in this world "too wonderful" for us to understand. Don't they all just point to our glorious, creative heavenly Father?

WHAT DO YOU THINK?

1. What is the single most awesome, jaw-dropping thing you have ever seen?

2. What else do you know about the eagle that sets it apart from all other birds?

3. Beside the point that these four items are amazing, what is the primary lesson in today's verses?

ANSWERS TO YOUR QUESTIONS

1. *Personal opinion. You may want to ask each child to think of a couple of things in their world that amaze them—like a shooting star or a hummingbird.*

2. *The eagle glides on air currents at over 40 MPH, but can dive vertically at 90 MPH or more. It feeds mainly on fish which it can snatch out of the water as it flies by—also rabbits and even deer fawn. The bald eagle is found all over North America including Mexico. Female eagles are 25% bigger than the males. They live about 20 years in the wild.*[13]

3. *God is the One who is truly awesome, because He made all animals, materials, and relationships. He has the most amazing imagination.*

97. IS YOUR NAME IN THE BOOK?

There are three things which are stately [majestic] in their march, even four which are stately when they walk: the lion which is mighty among beasts and does not retreat before any, the strutting cock [rooster], the male goat also, and a king when his army is with him.

Proverbs 30:29-31

Four stately things made it into today's proverb—a lion, a rooster, a goat, and a king with his army. In our world, many people strive to have their name written in a well-known book called *The Guinness Book of World Records*. They can achieve this by doing something bigger or faster (or more gross) than anyone else has done before.

What drives people to want to achieve a world record? Probably most people would like to be famous, even if they don't want a lot of public attention. Some may just want to prove to themselves that they can do one thing very well. Nobody may ever stop the person on the street and say, "Hey, aren't you the guy who ate a 12 inch pizza in one minute, 45 seconds on March 22, 2008?" But just knowing that his name is in *The Guinness Book of World Records* may help the fellow feel better about himself when he's having a down day.

Here are a few more interesting "firsts" from that book:

1. Youngest person to complete a marathon on all 7 continents – 23 years, 1/28/07
2. Most snow angels – 15,851 people, 2/02/04, London, Ontario, Canada
3. Largest gathering of Santa Clauses – 12,965, 9/09/07, N. Ireland
4. Longest lawnmower ride – 14,594.5 miles, finished 2/14/01, 9 ½ mos., 48 states and Mexico
5. Most rattlesnakes held in the mouth by the tail at one time – 10, 11/09/06, N.Y.
6. Most cockroaches eaten in one minute – 36, 3/05/01, London, England.[14]

These are fun facts, but *The Guinness Book of World Records* has nothing to do with eternity. In Revelation 21:27 we read about God's special book, the Lamb's Book of Life. For sure you want to find your name written there. Trying to break records won't achieve this. But when you trust Jesus as your Savior, the Bible says that God writes your name in His book. You are forever registered in heaven!

Now that's reason to be "stately" when you walk—the King of Kings has made you His child. You'll want to tell your family and friends about the Lamb's Book of Life, and how to make sure their names are written there too.

WHAT DO YOU THINK?

1. Why do you think many people want to break a world record and have their name written in *The Guinness Book of World Records*?

2. How do you go about getting your name written in the Lamb's Book of Life?

3. Who is *the Lamb,* and how did He get that name?

242

ANSWERS TO YOUR QUESTIONS

1. *Personal opinion. You may want to ask each child.*

2. *Jesus Christ has written every person's name in His book, who has believed that He died on the cross to pay for their sins, that He was buried, and that He rose again from the dead. The fact that the Father raised Jesus from the dead shows that our heavenly Father accepted Christ's sacrifice as sufficient payment for our sin.*

3. *In Old Testament times, God required the Jewish people to sacrifice a lamb without any defects, once a year. The high priest would take that blood and sprinkle it on the altar in the temple as a picture of Christ, who would one day give His life for the sins of the whole world. The Jewish sacrifices of lambs merely "covered over" the people's sins. Jesus was the Lamb of God who shed His own blood on the cross. His blood didn't just "cover" the sin of those who believed on Him; it "forgave and did away with" all of their sin forever.*

98. WHAT IS AN EXCELLENT WIFE?

An excellent wife, who can find? For her worth is far above jewels. The heart of her husband trusts in her, and he will have no lack of gain...She rises also while it is still night, and gives food to her household, and portions to her maidens.
Proverbs 31:10, 11, 15

It was almost supper time, and a hungry 15 year-old boy noticed that his mother was still lying down. Seized with concern—and hunger pangs—he said, "Mom, are you sick or something?"

"Well, as a matter of fact," his mother replied weakly, "I'm not feeling too well."

"I'm sorry, mom," the boy responded with furrowed brow. After a brief pause, he added, "Don't you worry a bit about dinner. I'm getting pretty big now and I'll be happy to carry you down to the kitchen!"[15]

When we begin to talk about a wife and mother, it's helpful to start with God's opinion. From today's verses we learn that He values a faithful wife much more than jewels. Some people like to rave about how rich people are who own many jewels, but a family is much richer when they realize the value of their godly wife and mother.

In many cultures around the world, women are not valued. A wife may be looked at like a piece of machinery that is expected to work hard, bear and raise children, keep gardens, provide food, and attend to her husband's needs. If for some reason the husband is displeased with his wife, it may be acceptable in his community to beat her, send her away, or take another wife or two, to make sure the work gets done.

But in Ephesians 5, which is written for married couples worldwide, the apostle Paul instructs, "Husbands, love your wives, just as Christ also loved the church and gave Himself up for her" (Ephesians 5:25). Wow! That sure sounds a lot different than treating your wife like a piece of machinery or a beast of burden. Because Jesus died for our sins, He wants husbands to love their wives with *His* love. It's an unselfish, caring kind of love. When children see their dad loving their mom, it's easier for them to love and honor her too.

Here are a few ideas to help you show your mom you love her:

- Be thankful for mom as a person, not just for what she *does* around the house.
- Take personal responsibility for keeping your room clean and tidy.
- Volunteer to do some of the many little jobs your mom does every day.
- Tell her regularly that you love her.
- Show your love as well as speak it.
- Check your attitude when you're tempted to argue with her.

What's the bottom line? You have a treasure in your home called "Mother."

WHAT DO YOU THINK?

1. Describe in your own words, what God says in today's verses about the value of a godly wife. Does a wife and mother have to be *perfect* in order to be valuable?

2. How can a husband love his wife the way God wants him to? How can he help his children to love and honor their mother?

3. When a dad loves Jesus first, and then seeks to love his wife as much as himself, what kind of family life do you think they might have? How would the kids feel?

ANSWERS TO YOUR QUESTIONS

1. *Personal opinion. Today's verses say that an excellent or godly wife is more valuable than jewels. She is a source of strength to her husband. She stays busy around the house from morning until night, caring for her family—and sometimes during the night. An excellent wife does not have to be perfect—only faithful to the Lord.*

2. *A husband needs to recognize that he cannot, by himself, love his wife fully. He should ask his heavenly Father to love his bride through him; then the Lord will do that. The children will easily see how much their dad loves their mom, and are more likely to give her the love and honor she deserves.*

3. *The children will see that their dad cares for their mother. He helps her when she's tired, sad, or upset. He does not yell at her. He is willing to stay home to help her at times when he'd previously planned to be out with his friends. He is thoughtful and creative in his words and actions. It's important to him that his children respect and obey their mom. His example helps the family want to get along well together and enjoy each other. The kids feel loved and secure.*

99. IT'S "MOM" APPRECIATION TIME

Strength and dignity are her clothing, and she smiles at the future. She opens her mouth in wisdom, and the teaching of kindness is on her tongue. She looks well to the ways of her household, and does not eat the bread of idleness.
Proverbs 31:25-27

God had a special purpose in mind when He created a woman (Eve) to be Adam's wife: "Then the Lord God said, 'It is not good for the man to be alone; I will make him a helper suitable for him'" (Genesis 2:18). Soon they became parents—and just like Eve, mothers are still busy caring for their families. How can you describe not only who mother *is*, but what she *does*?

The apostle Paul lists nine positive character qualities in Galatians 5:22, 23 that he calls the "fruit of the Spirit." These qualities help us describe a Christian wife and mother:

LOVE – "Mother love" is what causes a mom to get up out of bed in the middle of the night at her baby's first whimper. She will organize a fun birthday party for Junior, even when she's not feeling well. Mom also runs the best taxi service around.

JOY – A mother seems to get the greatest joy from the pleasure and success of her family—and she is often embarrassed when the attention turns to her.

PEACE – If world leaders truly wanted peace, I believe the United Nations would have a group of mothers get together. Who else referees more arguments?

LONGSUFFERING (also called patience) - Anyone who has carried a developing child inside them for nine long months without seeing it, has to be patient. And then she has to wait another twenty years to find out what kind of adult they'll be.

GENTLENESS – The Lord Jesus calls Himself "gentle" in Matthew 11:29. When a mother is guided by Him, she too will be selfless, kind-natured, and caring.

GOODNESS – No Christian mom would claim to be perfect, but she shows goodness in how she constantly trains her children to be the best they can be. She may even make the family pets toe the line.

FAITH – Moms who love Jesus, faithfully pray for their children. Where would the world be today without praying moms?

MEEKNESS – Meekness is not weakness! While a mother may quietly and humbly go about the care of her family and home, just let someone or something threaten to hurt her children. A mother's courage can be an amazing thing to behold when her family is endangered.

SELF-CONTROL – Mothers are great at multitasking. They are able to keep their minds on a variety of jobs and people at the same time. Yet, God has blessed moms with an amazing ability to focus—like, "Didn't I ask you last week to turn your socks right-side out, before putting them in the laundry?"

One of today's verses says it best: "She [mom] looks well to the ways of her household, and does not eat the bread of idleness" (Proverbs 31:27).

WHAT DO YOU THINK?

1. What reasons does God give for creating Eve?

2. Dad, Ask each child to share *two* areas where they see their mom's love for them personally or for the family in general. Help them to express their gratefulness to her.

3. Put the following sentence from today's verses in your own words: "She [mom] looks well to the ways of her household, and does not eat the bread of idleness."

ANSWERS TO YOUR QUESTIONS

1. *Adam needed the company of another person, because God said that it was not good for him to be alone. The first man also needed a "helper" who was "suitable" for him, or in other words, someone who was able to do or understand things that he could not.*

2. *Personal opinion. You may want to ask each child.*

3. *Personal opinion. The Christian mother who walks with God is faithful to focus on the care and well-being of her husband and children. She not only provides food, clothing, and a comfortable home; she also works diligently with her children to see them become fruitful servants for the Lord. There is no place for idleness or laziness in her life.*

100. THE FRAGRANCE OF WISDOM

Her children rise up and bless her; her husband also, and he praises her...Charm is deceitful and beauty is vain, but a woman who fears the Lord, she shall be praised.
Proverbs 31:28, 30

Congratulations! You have completed your journey through all one hundred devotionals. I hope you have come to value the wisdom that God gave Solomon and several others, and how He urged them to write those wise thoughts down for our benefit. By now we should realize the truth of the verse we read way back at the beginning: "The fear [loving awe, respect] of the Lord is the beginning of knowledge" (Proverbs 1:7).

When a Christian chooses to obey God, they experience Jesus' life bubbling up from within their soul and spirit. The Holy Spirit gives each believer the power to live for Jesus every day and at every stage of life.

Our verses for today talk about a woman's lasting beauty. It's not found in her eyes, her hair, or her facial features. True beauty that never fades over the years, but only increases, is that inner loveliness that only Jesus can produce. The apostle Paul says it so well when he writes, "But thanks be to God, Who in Christ always leads us in triumph [as trophies of Christ's victory] and through us spreads and makes evident the fragrance of the knowledge of God everywhere. *For we are the sweet fragrance of Christ...*" [The Amplified Bible] (2 Corinthians 2:14, 15a). As we walk with the Lord, we give off His fragrance wherever we go. How amazing is that!

Today's verses mention mother, father, and the children. I am so thankful to the Lord that your family is studying God's Word together. This was such an important part of our own family when our three children were growing up. Most nights after supper, we would sit in the living room and read a portion of the Bible, pray, and finish with a Christian adventure story for children.

We still talk about a humorous memory from a vacation trip to "Grandma's house." My wife was driving so I could read to our children, but we ran into a problem. We were going to reach Grandma's house before we finished the book, and we all wanted to know how the story ended. There was no turning back now. As we entered Grandma's town, we took a detour into a church parking lot and stayed there for an extra half hour while we finished the book.

All three of our children are married now with families of their own, and family devotions play an important role in each of their homes. Every parent would like to pass on part of their earthly treasure to their children and grandchildren. Material wealth changes daily with the stock market, but the sweet memories of "family times" around God's Word are eternal.

May our precious heavenly Father wrap His loving arms around you, comfort, inspire, and fill you with *the fragrance of His wisdom,* until the day you see Him face to face in the fullness of His glory!

WHAT DO YOU THINK?

1. The key verse of Proverbs seems to be, "The fear of the Lord is the beginning of knowledge; fools despise wisdom and instruction" (Proverbs 1:7). Does the first part of the verse mean that we should be scared or afraid of God in order to gain knowledge? What does "fear" mean in this verse?

2. Where does "true beauty" come from in a woman, and what is it?

3. What are some benefits for a family to have a daily time together to talk, read some Scripture, pray, and even read some other Christ-honoring books that are fun and adventurous?

ANSWERS TO YOUR QUESTIONS

1. *This verse can't mean that we should be afraid of God, because in verses like Isaiah 41:10, we are told not to be afraid. The word "fear" in Proverbs regarding God almost always means, "to reverence, hold in deep respect, consider to be awesome."*

2. *True beauty in a woman is not outward or physical. Such beauty changes over the years and youthful attractiveness fades into a more mature form. Inner or true beauty comes from the soul and spirit of a Christian woman which is the dwelling place of the Holy Spirit. As she obeys His guidance, the life of Christ bubbles up in her like a spring of fresh water, or the beautiful aroma of a rose.*

3. *Personal opinion. Some benefits of a family time are:*
   - *It brings honor to God.*
   - *It builds wonderful family memories that children will remember.*
   - *It gives parents an opportunity to teach their children about life.*
   - *It provides a relaxed time for kids to ask their questions.*
   - *It's a model for your children to follow when they become parents.*
   - *It teaches the importance of prayer and how God loves to answer.*

THEME INDEX

Theme	Devotion Number
Anger	49
Anger is sin	91
Animals – God's gift	36
Arguing	19
Arguing with God	70
Awesome God	96
Backsliding	48
Beauty	32
Bible	95
Boasting	81
Brave women	93
Brothers and sisters	59
Children, fathers, and granddads	58
Choices	83
Choosing friends	3
Christian America	50
Christ's sweet fragrance	100
Cool or fool	46
Correcting others	21
Counsel from God	39
Counselors	27
Courage and boldness	88
Creator God	11
Criticism or praise	12
Crooked minds	60
Crooked or righteous	13
Cursing	67
Deceit	20
Descendants	31
Discipline	10
Discipline	45
Disobedience	40
Drinking alcohol	68
Excellent Wife	98
Excellent Wife	35
Faithfulness	72

Faithful or unfaithful	82
Five senses	66
Foolish decisions	73
Fools	63
Future events	85
Generosity	33
Generous giving	9
God's book of names	97
God's guidance	15
God's promises	4
Good news	75
Gossip	57
Gossip	25
Gracious women	28
Guarding your heart	14
Happy homes	77
Hard work	16
Hard workers	87
Honesty	86
Honey and wisdom	78
Humility	62
Hurtful or helpful words	37
Hurtful words	69
Hurtful words	38
Integrity	23
Keeping your word	65
Kindness	5
Laziness	84
Love covers sins	24
Lying	18
Mom appreciation	99
Money	74
Mopey or cheerful	54
Nasty characters	71
Neighbors	26
Obedience produces happiness	92
Omnipresent God	52
Patience in hope	41
Planning	64
Pleasing God	30

Prayer   53
Pride   55
Pride   17
Questioning God   94
Rebellious children   90
Reputation of honesty   89
Reverence for God   2
Safe in God   61
Saving, giving, spending   44
Soft answer   51
Soul winning   34
Speaking appropriately   80
Stealing   29
Taught by Scripture   42
Teaching teens   76
Telling the truth   79
Trusting God   56
Trusting God   8
Trusting God or self   7
Truth   6
Wisdom   1
Wise and foolish   22
Wise or foolish   43
Witnessing for Jesus   47

NOTES

1. *My Way,* Songwriters: Revaux, Jacques; Anka, Paul (English lyrics); Thibaut, Gilles; Francois, Claude.

2. A. A. Milne, *Winnie-the-Pooh* (London: Methuen & Company Limited, 1926). Licensed to Walt Disney Productions in 1961.

3. *Hurricane Charley,* (August 9-15, 2004), Wikipedia, www.wikipedia.com, October, 2010.

4. *Tim Tebow,* Wikipedia, www.wikipedia.com, October, 2010.

5. *The Adventures of Ozzie and Harriet,* (ABC Television, 1952-1966), Wikipedia, www.wikipedia.com, October, 2010.

6. *Back to MSU Science Theatre Home Page,* Lansing State Journal, July 30, 1997.

7. Jill Carattini, *Cruciform Journey, a Slice of Infinity,* Ravi Zacharias International Ministries, February 22, 2010.

8. *Three-Toed Sloth,* Wikipedia, www.wikipedia.com, October, 2010.

9. *Audie Murphy,* Wikipedia, www.wikipedia.com, October, 2010.

10. *Pintos,* Bev Doolittle, Licensed by The Greenwich Workshop, Inc., www.greenwichworkshop.com.

11. Charles Ryrie, *Today in the World* (Chicago: MBI, December 1987), 7 – Quoted by www.bible.org.

12. *USS John F. Kennedy (CV-67),* Wikipedia, www.wikipedia.com, October, 2010.

13. *The Eagle,* Wikipedia, www.wikipedia.com, October, 2010.

14. Guinness World Records Limited, London, NW1 3HP, United Kingdom, http://www.guinnessworldrecords.com.

15. Daniel D. Meyer sermon, 5/11/2003. Quoted by *Leadership Weekly Newsletter, 5/04/2010, www.PreachingToday.com.*

DEAR READER........

Thank you for studying through these 100 devotionals from the book of Proverbs.

Our passion at Spring Glen Publishing is to encourage families to have a daily time together—even if it's short—where Jesus Christ is glorified through prayer, Bible reading, quality conversation, edifying books, and even singing choruses.

We would be thrilled if you would let us know if you have any questions, suggestions, comments, or creative ideas you discovered that make these devotionals more meaningful. And, of course, "How did your children enjoy them?"

Please contact us at:
SPRING GLEN PUBLISHING,
Box 530751,
Debary, FL   32753-0751
Tel. – 386-668-1569
Email – bryan@ComeRestWithMe.com
Web – www.SpringGlenPublishing.com

BOOK ORDERS:

If you would like to order copies, signed or unsigned, please contact us at the address above, or by Email. There are SPECIAL DISCOUNTS on the purchase of multiple copies for Bible study groups, classes, and gifts.

Are you looking for

sound, Biblical, devotional material for your own study? For your small group? For resource material?